The

United States-

Mexico

Border

A POLITICO-ECONOMIC PROFILE

by
Raul A. Fernandez

UNIVERSITY OF NOTRE DAME PRESS
NOTRE DAME   LONDON

Copyright © 1977 by
University of Notre Dame Press
Notre Dame, Indiana 46556

Library of Congress Cataloging in Publication Data

Fernandez, Raul A   1945–
  The United States-Mexico border.

  1. Southwest, New—Economic conditions.   2. Texas—
Economic conditions.   3. Mexico—Economic conditions.
I. Title.
HC107.A165F47   330.9′764   76–22409
ISBN 0–268–01914–2

Manufactured in the United States of America

Contents

v

The United States–
Mexico Border

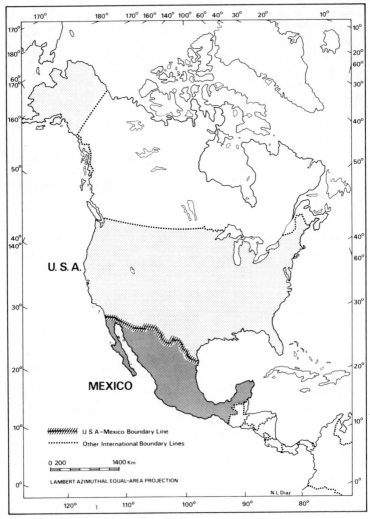

Mexico and the North American Continent

Introduction

This book is a study of the political economy of the United States-Mexico border region. Some specialists may not be impressed with my method of presentation and analysis. Historians may find themselves uninspired by the dearth of *new* historical data. With the exception of the last three chapters, much of the material utilized has appeared in print before. On the other hand, "traditional" economists may view my effort to expand the understanding of current economic developments on the Mexican border via a historical examination as fruitless. The task I have set is that of organizing and giving coherence, with the aid of theory, to a body of historical data already, for the most part, available.

My theoretical conviction is that a realistic quantitative and qualitative determination of economic systems aimed at specifying *conditions for change* cannot be arrived at by using the ahistorical tools and concepts of "neoclassical economic theory." Rather, any such attempt must incorporate institutional and historical elements. The extreme formalization of neoclassical models and their emphasis on characteristics which are common to all economic systems, rather than those which are peculiar to each, have obscured an understanding of the process of social change and development. More correctly, the shortcomings of economic "science" arise from the reduction of "sociology" to individuals; the reduction of "psychology" to rational calculation; the determination that society is a harmonious whole; and the equation of class differences with differences in innate individual talent.

The tight molds imposed by the implicit societal assumptions of neoclassical theory have become more and more of an obstacle in the minds of a generation of young economists who recognize that the "sociology" and "politics" of an adequate economic science must pass beyond "individual consumers" and "G" (government). The concept of the individual consumer is itself a historical product. So, an economic science that purports to be general in its scope cannot impose concepts based on the notion of "individuals" in societies where the concept is not present in concrete reality. Similarly, the narrowness of rational calculation—so central to the "psychology" of modern economic theory—has come under widespread attack. One of the graver consequences of this formal reductionism is the freedom of the "theorist" to collect data (numbers) based on the given taxonomy and to statiscize the result. A contemporary example of this practice is the recent flood of literature showing the superiority of white over nonwhite students on the basis of something that is measurable, i.e., intelligence. This crude empiricism—rampant in economics and in the "other" social sciences—is the result of an unfortunate confusion between what is factual and what is truthful.

Social forces more complex than the ones depicted in formal models have been at work in the process of emphasizing formalization, statistization, etc. During the last two decades, the social sciences have engaged in a race to be classified as "hard sciences." Part of this tendency has been motivated by the orientation of fund-granting agencies in the United States: the road to formalization and statistization has been cleared by the availability of funds for the support of this type of research. The consequence is that a pecking order has been established with the "harder"—or more formal—disciplines at the top and with everyone vying for first place. In this manner a form of curricular imperialism of the most pedantic kind has become fashionable, with economics as its standard bearer. Within each discipline the result has been a ridiculous and destructive separation of professionals into "hard heads" and "soft heads," with obvious connotations. This separation parallels the confusion between the ability to collect statistics and the production of meaningful results. The implied rationale is that capacity to quantify concepts and operations places the social sciences on a par with the physical sciences.

These pitfalls of the social sciences have rendered social science incapable of understanding the economic plight of racial minorities in the United States. Years of sociological, psychological, political, and geographical research into the conditions of Mexican Americans, for example, has not shed much light on the social origins and persistence of their plight, much less provided solutions to their problems.

II

I hope to demonstrate that the study of the process of economic change in and around the border area between Mexico and the United States is a topical as well as an authentic area of social scientific inquiry. In brief, an adequate study of the history of the border economic processes must shed some additional light on the determination of the economic systems of the two countries as well as the economic and political relations between them.

The boundary between the United States and Mexico is unique for a variety of reasons. The first important contemporary characteristic is the development of a string of population centers extending from the Gulf of Mexico to the Pacific Ocean usually named "border towns." This denomination is almost never applied to any of the population centers on the American-Canadian border; in fact, the American-Canadian border is, more often than not, referred to as the "boundary." The word "border," and especially the phrase "border town," has negative connotations which imply conditions of unsettlement and hostility. Additionally, the population concentration in the area is far from an ordinary situation: the area that is called northern Mexico has had the highest population growth rate of any region its size since the mid-fifties.

A second factor which makes the presence of these cities somewhat incongruous is their origin: the border towns appear to have no other economic-geographic raison d'être than the fact that they were set up as cross points on the border line. With few exceptions (El Paso–Juarez being perhaps the most important), the cities that are called border towns defy the canons of economic-geographic location theory and owe their existence quite literally to the existence of the border line.

The Mexican border is a unique contemporary example of the contrast between rich and poor nations or, as it has commonly been put, between "developed" and "underdeveloped" nations. Above and beyond the particularities of this situation, the adjacency of these two nations may serve to illustrate and perhaps to emphasize in a manner not obvious in other situations, the kinds of ties that have developed and are developing between advanced and backward nations. This example may also serve to illustrate forcefully such a relationship's projected path of development.

Thirdly, the study of this area cannot avoid two historically crucial developments: the expansion and conquest (1836–48) of a large area of Mexican territory by the United States; and a continuous saturation of the southwestern states by Mexican immigration, especially since the turn of the century. I will show that this latter development is clearly bound up with the adjacency of two vastly different socio-economic fabrics and, as such, it is unique although not without historical precedent. Although it is impossible to disregard direct and indirect references to the situation of the Chicano population of the Southwest, the methodology used does not allow an interpretation of Chicano history based on cultural difference or cultural oppression.

Meaningful research and analysis that guides subsequent political and social action must be grounded on the material forces and social relations of production which ultimately define the historical course of any group of people. To remain at a level of explanation which blames one racial or cultural group for having committed cultural genocide meets the requirements for moral indignation, but goes no further. Indeed, such methodology leads to the conclusion that the history of mankind is nothing but "an erratic series of cultural genocides."

To proceed with this kind of approach can lead into several blind alleys: one would be the assumption of complete cynicism at the "horrible pageant" of mankind and the taking of an ahistorical, "existential" posture with regard to the "evil nature of man"; another one would be the acquisition of a spiritual satisfaction based on the philosophical notion that "one's culture is as good as that of the white man's," regardless of the facts of oppression. A third road is traveled by a social strategy characterized by moralistic idealism where the slogan would be that all nations (which are viewed as equivalent to cultures) have equal rights to exist in a sovereign way, regardless of their concrete historical character; that is, regardless of the fact that "nations" are not eternal entities. A colony, or a nation, is a sensible concept when it is rooted in real material and historical circumstances, but not when it only serves a rhetorical purpose. Therefore, one must ask whether it makes sense to speak of a colony or a nation in relation to the Chicano people. Does it have a defined territory or an economy of its own? In what sense is it possible to speak of a nation during the present epoch, i.e., is a Chicano nation going to fulfill the historical role of nation-states in previous centuries?

III

The methodology that I utilize is that of historical materialism. The fundamental aspect of historical materialism is that the development of the history of mankind depends on the development of the contradictions between the forces of production and the social relations of production, on the material conditions of life (base or mode of production), and on its ideological conceptions (superstructure). Classical Marxism endeavored to determine the fundamental features of capital-

ism, and to demonstrate that it was a historical mode of production that arose in a determinate historical moment; that
capitalism embodied inherent contradictions which would
eventually destroy and transform it into a different mode of
production; and that capitalism manifested specific traits
which distinguish it from previous forms of social production.
The backbone of Marxist social theory is that the critic can
arrive by way of the theory of successive modes of production
at a correct analysis of classes in a concrete situation.

This constitutes the theoretical framework, or the "paradigm," that is adopted here. The application of this general
theoretical framework to the concrete case of the United
States-Mexico border area should concern the delineation of
modes of production coexisting side by side within a unified
economic system. For this reason, I have placed a special
emphasis on the analysis of feudal remnants in land tenure late
in the nineteenth century in the otherwise capitalistic Southwest. Secondly, it is crucial to identify the specific manifestations of the development of monopoly capitalism in the border
area, an aspect that is emphasized in the analysis of migration.
Finally, I have attempted to show the importance of the relationships which arise from the uneven economic development
of different social formations. Although I have not attempted
to write a "history" of the border area, the chapters are written
in an order which implies a certain chronology and periodiza-
tion.

The First Stage

The first period extends from 1848 (or 1836 in the case of
Texas) to approximately the turn of the century. This early
stage is characterized by the head-on collision between two
different socio-economic formations. The social economy that
was predominant in the northwestern part of Mexico during
the Spanish and Mexican periods can best be described as a
variant of feudalism. This is true in terms of class relations
(basically *patrones* and *peones*), in terms of the forms of

economic border. The present stage is one where the legal border is, in *some* ways, a fiction, and has been left behind by the advance of the integration process. This rapid movement is part and parcel of a new dimension of the international business scene usually referred to as "the rise of the multinationals," "worldwide sourcing and dedomiciling," etc. This is an ongoing process, manifesting itself in a veritable mass exodus of labor-intensive industries from the developed countries into low-wage developing ones.

The multinational corporation, or "the highest stage of corporate development," came into the United States-Mexico border area in the form of the Border Industrial Program (BIP), which was instituted in 1965 and was in full operation in 1967. The primordial role that the BIP was supposed to assume was the alleviation of widespread unemployment prevalent along the 2,000 mile common border with the United States. The Border Industrial Program is, today, no longer limited to the border, and there are numerous plants in other states, such as Yucatán and Aguascalientes.

As the economic border progresses beyond the international line, the effects of this international line are still felt. Once again, a phenomenon of unique dimensions has appeared in this area of the world: the border town. It has already been pointed out that we hardly ever refer to cities on the international boundary with Canada or, for that matter, to cities on international borders in other parts of the world as border towns. The occurrence of a "border town" is brought about by a host of factors, the principal one being the contrasts which exist between the two countries facing each other across this line.

The present border area and the border towns included in it are continuing the trends of rapid growth, urban sprawl, high unemployment, and squalor experienced during the 1950s and 1960s. The economy of these towns is increasingly shaped by the presence of American industry, the transport of vegetables northward, the flow of tourists southward, the flow in both directions of contraband items (including weapons), the flourishing of prostitution, and the dynamics of illegal traffic in hard drugs. These items effect a deepening of the elements of social cleavage and the disruptions already present in this semimodern, semibackward atmosphere.

i: Material Basis of Culture in the Old Borderlands

What was the operative system of social economy in New Mexico and California during the Anglo conquest, and how had it evolved from Oñate's early *entrada* of the late 1500s? This chapter attempts to sketch the requirements of a minimal answer to that query and further seeks to specify the direction of internal change within this social fabric.

In analyzing patterns of social change and social structure in New Mexico, it is necessary to mention two stages of colonization, which can be separated by the Pueblo Revolt of the 1680s. During the first hundred years of colonization, the Spanish arrivals in New Mexico basically applied the same approach to the Pueblo Indians that had been implemented elsewhere in New Spain (Mexico). As such, the conquest of New Mexico forged the last link in a northward chain of conquest and colonization. The social relations of production which the Spanish colonists ideally desired to construct in the new territory were contained in the proposal advanced by one of the candidates considered by the Crown for the colonization project. Juan Bautista de Lomas y Colmenares, a rich miner from the Zacatecas region, asked for: the title of *adelantado* for his family in perpetuity as well as the appointment of governor-captaincy for six generations; the prerogative to bestow three *encomiendas* in perpetuity as well as any others for six generations; forty thousand vassals in perpetuity with attendant rights to the lands, water, and woods under their jurisdiction; a nobiliary title such as count or marquess; a ten-year monopoly on the raising of livestock in the region; and a few other items. This proposal was accepted in principle by the viceroy in Mexico. Even though he was empowered to authorize it, the viceroy, beset by inner doubt or scruple, forwarded the proposal to the king who refused to authorize it.[1] The fact that a request almost entailing the creation of a new sovereign principality could be seriously considered reflects two aspects of colonization in New Spain. As colonization progressed towards the northern frontier of New Spain, the royal authorities came to rely more and more heavily on colonists wealthy enough to effect the process. On the other side of the coin, this process allowed the more prosperous colonists an increasing power to acquire and develop enormous estates. These estates—or *latifundios*—became the norm of land tenure in northern New Spain during the sixteenth and seventeenth centuries.

When the conquest of New Mexico had been effected, *encomiendas* and *repartimientos* formed the basis of colonial production. As an institution, the encomienda dates back to the colonization of Castile during the retreat of the Moors.[2] Its appearance in New Mexico reflects the traditional assignments granted to a Spanish conqueror—in this case to some of Oñate's top soldiers—of supervision over land near an Indian community whose population was required to perform labor on these lands for the benefit of the encomendero.

Additionally, large landgrants were given to the more prominant Spaniards. Through the encomiendas, the Pueblo villages contributed an annual tribute in kind to the leading colonists, usually consisting of maize and cotton blankets. The repartimiento—or apportionment of labor required from the Indian population living near an encomienda—was utilized to the fullest extent by the settlers living on farms and ranches. Although a nominal sum of money was expected in exchange for Indian labor, there is enough evidence to suggest that the colonists did not comply with this requirement but, rather, simply appropriated the fruits of coerced, enforced labor. During the early years of the encomienda's development in

New Spain, the distribution of labor, and not necessarily the distribution of land, influenced the placement of encomiendas. Consequently, defined boundaries between encomiendas did not exist and, with the exhaustion of precious metals, some of the early encomiendas were transformed into large farm estates.

The encomiendas and repartimientos required the native inhabitants to till the soil, tend livestock, work in mines, and carry burdens in addition to the obligatory tribute. In New Mexico, there was little question of mining after initial explorations demonstrated the absence of gold or silver and, as a result, New Mexico was not characterized by the opulence and splendor that had typified earlier outposts such as Zacatecas. The general relative poverty of the New Mexico colony has led to questioning the view that here as well as elsewhere Spanish Mexicans lived comfortably off the coerced labor of their Indian serfs.[3] A number of problems are involved in this issue: first, though the tribute accruing from the encomienda did not amount to much, coerced repartimiento labor was clearly of greater economic importance to the Spanish-Mexican settlers. Here, as well as elsewhere in New Spain, the colonists lived off the labor of their Indian charges. Whether they lived *comfortably* or not is an outside conditioning factor which does not alter the pattern of subjection characteristic of the society.

The social relations of the early New Mexican province were feudal in character. Historically, feudal or tributary societies emerged at a time when the development of production and the degree of human knowledge and control of natural forces were at a fairly undeveloped level. Consequently, natural catastrophes affected every member of the society, regardless of class, rank, or status. Plagues and drought were the natural enemies of European feudal systems; the absence of rich minerals in New Mexico and its position as a weak frontier outpost surrounded by a hostile environment made this society poor as a whole, but did not eliminate class relations.

In feudal societies, the need to cooperate against the forces of nature, and the physical proximity due to geographical isolation (lack of development of means of transport) bred a definite form of paternalism where the lord truly cared for his vassals and serfs. This aspect of precapitalist society was, of course, reinforced by tenets of religious alienation which rationalized the modus vivendi. The nature of class relations in precapitalist societies can be favorably compared (from a romantic point of view) with the atomization and competitive mentality prevalent in a fully developed capitalist society. In this light, it is possible to refer to the "benevolence" of feudalism as specifically superior to that of capitalism.[4] Social *analysis*, however, should strive to look not only at the daily exposition of benevolence or lack thereof, but at the long-term path of a society's development, and at the material chances of escape from a position of coerced servitude. In feudal situations, then, benevolence may be viewed as an instrument of continued domination, and not as an idyllic virtue from older, better times.

In the case of New Mexico, the question becomes academic. Raids by nomadic tribes and disease decimated the Pueblos after 1665. With their numbers depleted, the labor requirements of the Spaniards became harder and harder to meet. Finally, the Pueblos rose in revolt in 1680, exterminated most of the colonists, and drove the survivors out of the upper Rio Grande Valley for the next twelve years.

The revolt of the Pueblos aborted a process of development in land tenure patterns that had spread over all of Mexico by the end of the seventeenth century. This process can be described as an official sanctioning—embodied in property rights—of the results of a trend toward indiscriminate use of land present from the beginning of the Conquest. In the sixteenth century, the process of land occupation in New Spain had been highly irregular. The only consistent characteristics of land occupation were the drive to acquire larger and larger portions of land; the appropriation and stewardship of communal Indian lands; and the stockmen's use of grazing lands, usually available to all inhabitants of a town. By the beginning of the seventeenth century, Mexico had experienced a de facto division into a conglomeration of extensive estates primarily devoted to cattle and sheep raising. Throughout the seventeenth century, this subdivision became legally sanctioned: the obligatory settlement of land titles became a new source of revenue for military expenditures in the eyes of the Spanish sovereign, and a tax was levied upon the newly required settlement of property. This measure was fought by most landholders since it directly affected their pockets, but in the long run, and despite erstwhile monetary impoverishment, the status and predominance of the large estate was secured. While in most of New Spain, landholders were obligated during the seventeenth century to define and legalize their property, the settlers in the northern provinces were specifically exempted because of frontier conditions.[5] This whole process came to a grinding halt in New Mexico. This is not the whole story on the formation of large estates in Mexico, but we will have occasion to return to this point later.

Twelve years after the Pueblo Revolt, the Spanish Mexicans returned to the upper Rio Grande Valley. At this time, Spanish landgrants became of prime importance in the history of the borderlands. However, the significance of the Spanish land-grant system has usually been approached a posteriori, i.e., via the violations of Spanish juridical systems that Anglo invaders effected. No adequate examination has been made either of the influence of the land tenure system on the internal dynamics of Hispanic society in the Southwest or of the internal variations that occurred from area to area. The fact that the society of the Southwest was conquered by an alien nation, and that the resulting cultural conflict became explicit in many ways (one of them being the struggle over land titles) has deterred attention to possibly conflicting elements in patterns of land tenure and other, concommitant economic peculiarities in the two opposing societies. Had Hispanic land titles been recognized and respected, would this land tenure system have survived the impact of the invader's institutions? The answer to this question entails an investigation of the property relations prevailing in New Mexico during the eighteenth century.

The Spanish crown (and later the Mexican government) allowed three types of landgrants in the northern provinces:

individual grants given to important people or sold to those with financial means, joint grants to groups of individuals, and community grants given to a group of settlers. Relatively few individual grants were issued during the Spanish period in New Mexico, and those usually went to prominent citizens. Joint grants were usually issued to a group of families who were generally accompanied by a larger group of families and individuals. In the main, the initial grantees allowed the accompanying people small residential lots and small portions of irrigable land to cultivate. These people usually provided the bulk of the labor force required by the initial grantees, who were usually engaged in livestock production. In town or community grants, land was allocated in three forms to each settler: residential lots, farming or irrigable lands, and common land, usually for grazing purposes. The particular topography of the terrain dictated the layout of most farmsteads in thin strips of land on both banks of the Rio Grande.[6] The incentive to stay close to one's farmland, and the absence of fertile soil and/or water away from the river generated a string of small strips farther and farther along the banks of the river. This situation eventually had a dispersal effect on the towns of early New Mexico, despite the constant threat of hostile Indians. It also yielded the phenomenon of squatting in the outlying areas.

From this very basic outline of land distribution in eighteenth-century New Mexico, what can we say about the social relations that emanated from it? Some speculation leans toward the view that the legal apparatus was a model of judicial wisdom since it granted some land proprietorship to the poor as well as to the rich.[7] Additionally, this view suggests that town and joint grants provided an important stimulus for communalism by making some of the building and defensive tasks obligatory for everyone. Empirically, of course, this kind of analysis is utopian and romantic in the extreme. During the eighteenth and nineteenth centuries, the colonized area of New Mexico became characterized by the presence of two basic classes—the patrones and the peones. The patrones were not only those holders of individual grants who chose to include servants in their holdings; it seems that in many villages, the *realengos* (common lands) designed for the pasturage of every neighbor came to be generally utilized by two or three large livestock owners in the village. The rest of the settlers became laborers in their de facto haciendas and, occasionally, kept some cattle themselves. The livestock owners became the patrones upon whom the majority of others were dependent for work.

To understand the transition from early settlements which appeared to have a more varied stratification to the simple pattern that resulted, one must look at two aspects of their social formation: first, the nature and tendencies of small, agricultural farmsteads within the larger social formation and, second, the history of the relationship between stock raising and agriculture in this mode of production.

From the beginning of the allocation of land, the small tiller was doomed to eke out little more than subsistence from his plot. The amount of land that he could cultivate was regulated by law, and the absence of primogeniture rights made the size of the plots decrease over generations. Given the availability of water and the degree of technical development, there was simply little possibility for the expansion of agricultural production toward larger areas away from the river. These factors were bound to prevent the expansion of agriculture, either in an extensive sense, or in the sense of gradual improvements in yield due to the application of more sophisticated scientific farming. The small proprietor could, at best, succeed in maintaining his rights of property; in the end, he generally became indebted and secured his livelihood by laboring on the large ranches. His formal independence and, in some cases, his property ownership, were hardly conducive to further economic growth.

The subjection of the small tiller by large ranchers occurs in New Mexico and, in this sense, there is considerable similarity to the process that established the large haciendas and the patron-peon relationship in northern Mexico. Earlier, we described the events leading to the de jure consolidation of the large estates (haciendas) in New Spain during the seventeenth century, but the de facto build-up of such large estates was only hinted at.

From the beginning of colonization in New Spain, colonial laws and regulations attempted to contain any desire for independent fiefdoms that might arise from the possession of large areas of land. Within a century of the Conquest, however, the economy of New Spain had become highly dependent on stock raising, and this dependence led to the formation of the large Mexican hacienda. A number of reasons have been advanced for the growth of cattle raising in Mexico. One initial—and purely functional factor—was the service that cattle haciendas provided for the mining centers in terms of the basic supplies of meat, animals, and hides. A second factor was, certainly, the tremendous demographic toll Mexico took in the sixteenth century, which severely restricted the availability of manual labor. Stock raising was favorably viewed because of its low labor requirements.[8]

Despite regulations that appeared to restrict the development of large estates, Mexico suffered the same fate in this regard as Spain. The stock raisers' growing power allowed them to make a sham of existing regulations by conniving with municipal authorities—other cattle raisers—to secure their private use of common pasture lands. Even though the viceroy tried, at first, to interfere, the process was too massive to be contained. For a time, the stock raisers maintained an appearance of respect for the integrity of the law while, through their association, the *Mesta,* they worked out the details of their private use of common lands.[9] Coupled with this was the tremendous numerical growth of cattle and sheep in the entire region during the first hundred years of conquest, a biological wonder due to the untouched pastures of Mexico. The growth of cattle caused the destruction of Indian farmlands, and in turn caused an abandonment of villages and whole valleys by the dispossessed local population during the sixteenth century. This phenomenon can easily be compared with a foreign invasion or a natural disaster. Numerous abuses also arose from the old Spanish practice of allowing cattle to graze on crop fields after the harvest was completed.

By the time a pasture-cattle equilibrium had been reached, the haciendas held an entrenched position; mining dropped back in the ranks of economic activities, and former miners turned into wealthy stockmen. This pattern also emerged in northern Mexico where it was reinforced by the tendency of the central Spanish government to rely on rich men to carry out the initial colonization project. Extensive areas of northern Mexico were populated by large flocks in the seventeenth century. The process which elevated stock raisers into a position of undisputed dominance in New Mexico was roughly similar to the process that had occurred earlier farther to the south.

Certainly, different areas of New Mexico were characterized by different degrees of patron and livestock raiser predominance.[10] Even in the case of New Spain, it is not true to claim that the hacienda penetrated every aspect of the social system, since whole areas—such as the valley of Oaxaca—were different in structure. Still, hacienda formation was the dominant and decisive one. Thus, in New Mexico the patron-peon relationship was, empirically and tendentially, also the dominant pattern of social relations, although it was obviously not the only one.

Doubts on this score have been cast by reports indicating that people of all classes enjoyed a substantial diet of animal meat. To confuse the ability of a social formation to feed or not feed all its members at a certain point in time says little about the social relations and the direction of change. It is well known, for instance, that some groups of African hunters and gatherers consume considerably more meat on a daily basis than the average European or American—in fact, the designation the "original affluent society" has been coined for this situation.[11] In the fourteenth century, the citizens of Frankfurt enjoyed a diet of meat and poultry that has been unequaled since.[12] What can we infer about social relations from these material facts other than that they are contingent factors?

A specific instance of the development of patron-peon relationships in New Mexico is the *partido* system. This system began in the late eighteenth century and remained in effect until the beginning of the twentieth century. Its life course seems to have been closely tied to the life cycle of the area's sheep industry. Basically, the livestock proprietor would turn over a breeding herd to a tenant. The renter was bound to return twenty lambs for every hundred ewes in the original group at the end of a year. The lessee also rented rams, sold the lambs and wool through the owner, and was responsible for any losses and the usual costs of operation. He was also obliged to return, upon demand, a breeding herd of the same size and age as the one he had originally obtained. The tenant received the proceeds of the sale of wool, the excess lambs, and grazing rights on the owner's lands for all sheep under his supervision (at a specified rate, of course). As such, the partido system held little hope for small independent livestock operators. Based upon the existing control of grazing resources, its stipulations were intended to maintain the separation between large and small owners.[13]

A good deal of sociability developed, in New Mexico during the colonial period, especially among the rich. The large, extended families saw a good deal of each other and interclass relations were personal in nature. What local changes were brought about by Mexico's independence from Spain? In the very basic sense of social production that we have spoken about—the foundation of social relations on the ownership of productive resources—the sheep industry's tendency towards predominance intensified and began to expand its area of operation. During the Mexican era, the migration pattern followed the movement of large flocks of sheep. Much more evidence is available on the development of patron and partido systems during this time. The Mexican government advanced the process of settlement, and a sizable number of large individual grants were issued during this period. Mexican independence, then, provided additional stimulus to the area's land-based dominant class and an expansion of its domain.

California was another major area of Hispanic conquest and colonization in the Southwest. In California, as in New Mexico and parts of Texas and Arizona which were occupied at this time, stock raising became a principal item of material production.[14]

Within this common denominator of economic production, some differences of timing in development of similar social relations of production emerged, especially between California and New Mexico. California history shows a different chronology from that of New Mexico.[15] When the colonization of California began in earnest, the New Mexico settlement could claim a history of two hundred years. The reasons for this late colonization were very specific, and were apparently concerned with the fears of the Spanish crown regarding the possible intrusion of Russians and even Englishmen in the territory.[16] At any rate, the colonization of California began in the last third of the eighteenth century.

Although the legal history of property relations in the California settlement is very similar in form to that of its older cousin to the east, its content varies considerably. To begin with, the Spanish government granted very few landgrants of any size to individual settlers. So conservative was the Spanish government, that between the year 1782 and the end of the Spanish period, only twenty individual landgrants had been issued. The other side of this situation was the tremendous role, and land control exercised by the "mission system" in California during these years and well into the Mexican period. This system, as it developed in California was never known in New Mexico. From the founding of the first New Mexican mission—the mission of Friar Ruiz in Puaray in 1581—through the subsequent founding of numerous others, their role in New Mexico was almost imperceptible.

In carrying out its assignments to introduce New World Indians to Christianity as well as European culture, the Roman Catholic Church depended upon the effectiveness of its missionaries who belonged to various religious orders. They were as aggressive in their spiritual conquest as the soldiers had been in their physical conquest. Almost from the beginning, the Church accompanied the invading forces in the Southwest; each expedition numbered priests among its members. As soon as a territory was settled, Jesuits (and later Franciscans) took up residence and began their work among the colonists and Indians. None of the clerics seems to have questioned the legitimacy of Spanish rule in the Southwest, although early in the Conquest the Christian voice was the only one raised against the cruelty of the encomienda and repartimiento.[17]

The Jesuit order was responsible for the first missions in the Southwest. The Jesuits were characterized as being well-organized and militant, with an efficiency that yielded economic power. Their success aroused the jealousy of other orders as well as the suspicion of the Crown. The king of Spain, protective of his power, had the Jesuits expelled from the New World colony in 1760, and replaced them with the Franciscans, an order somewhat more harmonious with the Spanish absolutism of the eighteenth century.[18]

In general, the relations between Church and state in the New World were sufficiently harmonious to allow the Church to become quite wealthy. Having seemingly converted numerous Indians in the sixteenth century, the Church became involved in other matters, notably, the acquisition of property and wealth. Tithes and parochial fees provided a small share of the Church's income: the principal source of wealth was furnished by legacy. The wealthy were expected to leave part of their wealth to the Church when they died. Not leaving a legacy for the convents constituted an immoral, irreligious act, and this sin of omission placed the soul's final salvation in jeopardy. Over the decades, the Church accumulated vast estates. Banks were extremely rare and the ruling groups had little liquid capital, but loans could be obtained from the monasteries.[19]

Nowhere was the influence of the mission felt as in California, where, in 1822, the Church held the largest portion of desirable land and, consequently, almost all the livestock. What kind of social organization was adopted by the Franciscan missionaries to administer this wealth? What historical role did this power and social organization play in the long run? The missionaries of California confronted a different situation than those in New Mexico. In New Mexico, as in large parts of

Mexico and South America, the Indian population was concentrated in native towns and villages and the missionaries were able to take the faith to them. In contrast, the California Indians were dispersed, and the missionaries were compelled to bring them to the faith under the cover of the mission and its adjoining lands. This measure permitted the maximum use of a few clergymen in the administration and supervision of the Indians. The center of each mission was a church or chapel, built by the doubtful converts. Surrounding the church were the living quarters, schools, warehouses, and prison facilities for unruly Indians. Mass was a daily procedural requirement, after which the Indians went to work in the fields from sunrise to sunset.[20] Once the Indian had been brought into the mission on whatever pretext and once he evidenced the vaguest tendency toward conversion, he became a virtual slave whose contact with his pagan relatives was to be prevented at all costs.[21]

Under the mission system, the California Indians were clearly subjected to coerced, compulsory labor which bore a striking resemblance to slavery. The neophytes performed physical labor in handicraft production, agriculture, and construction. While mission work was not exorbitantly strenuous, this qualitative aspect of labor must be viewed in terms of the missionaries' primary objective to keep Indian recruits continuously occupied. The Indians were not spared brutality and arduous work, however, because in addition to the tasks performed on mission lands, neophytes were "loaned" out to work in the presidios and for individual Spanish soldiers. While the Indians were supposed to receive some remuneration for this work, in fact they received no payment for their labor. In this capacity, the Indians performed a number of tasks, ranging from errand boy and cowboy to ditch-digger, i.e., they did all the work the soldiers were supposed to do.[22]

The mission system was basically a series of concentration camps where Indians were relocated for the purpose of providing labor services and for the destruction of their native religious beliefs. While some Indians acquired certain skills, the mission system failed to prepare the vast majority for an existence beyond the scope of their native culture. This occurred not necessarily because of the evil intentions of Franciscan monks, but because the mission—as a conductor of a mode of material production which developed in Spain and later in Mexico—was not adequately equipped to do otherwise.

Economic life within the mission compound revolved around the somewhat mutually exclusive constraints of discipline and productivity. While the padres were concerned about introducing domestic animals and cultivatable products to make the missions self-sufficient, this was a short-term goal tempered, in the long run, by the need to maintain a strict level of discipline and spiritual advancement. To develop individual skills to a maximum degree and to attempt the achievement of a high volume of production would have run counter to the mission's idea of spiritual advancement.[23]

In California, the missionaries never held titles to the land they acquired, nor did they apparently envision its appropriation by the order. However, since specific social and physical conditions motivated considerable expansion of the de facto use of the best lands, little else was left for lay individuals. To illustrate this phenomenon, it is sufficient to mention two instances of territorial expansion. The grazing lands of San Gabriel Mission, although not contiguous, extended from the pueblo of Los Angeles to the mouth of the San Gabriel and Santa Ana rivers, and eastward through La Puente, Santa Ana del Chino, Jurupa, San Bernardino, and San Gorgonio—a total distance close to seventy miles. In the north, the grazing lands of Mission San Carlos extended from Carmel Valley and its surrounding hills and mountains—as well as from the mouth of the Salinas River—up to Chualar.

The expanse of mission livestock range and wealth made it difficult to attract new settlers to the area. As a result, the mission system came under incessant scrutiny during the Mexican period. It appears that the padres were a fairly insignificant political obstacle. Thus, the mission system came to an end in 1833 with the secularization and distribution of its land and livestock holdings to private landgrant holders. The secularization of mission lands marked the second major period (pre-1848) in the history of land tenure practices and social relations in California—the era of the *ranchos*.[24]

Few colonists had settled in California before 1822, and only thirteen new grants were made by the Mexican government between 1822 and 1833. After the secularization of mission lands, a massive process of carving up the area began. Between 1833 and 1846, approximately eight hundred new grants involving upwards of 8 million acres of the best land were distributed at a feverish pace. Property in land and its accompanying livestock became so highly concentrated that, by 1848, it is estimated that forty individuals held virtually absolute control over the economic and political affairs of California.

In California, the predominant economic unit was transferred overnight from the Franciscan mission to the rancho. The size and number of these ranchos and the social relations they engendered became important for several decades. The institution of the rancho has been traditionally compared with that of the medieval English manor. Each rancho was, to a large extent, self-sufficient. Even though a great deal of production related to livestock was utilized for export purposes, these exports satisfied the luxury needs of the ranchos and did not play a significant role in the daily reproduction of life.[25]

If the institution of the rancho has been compared with the English feudal manor, the generalized social relations that accompanied it have been likened to the slave South. During the mission system, the predominant forms of labor were religious forced-labor and peonage in the presidios. As the ranchos became organized, a situation closely resembling that of New Mexico developed with a small, solid, landed aristocracy at the top and a mass of former mission Indians at the bottom. Paraphrasing a ranchero, the Indian tilled the soil, pastured cattle, sheared sheep, cut timber, built houses, paddled boats, made bricks and tiles, ground grain, slaughtered cattle, and dressed their hides for market, while Indian women worked as servants, brought up the children, and cooked every meal. Was this not slavery?

In California, a form of debt-peonage also became operative

during this period. Before an Indian could move from place to place, he was required to prove that he had been legally discharged by and was not in debt to his employer. This practice persists and indeed typifies the relationship of many contemporary South American rural landowners to their servants of the land. In addition to this veiled, coercive apparatus designed to secure a stable labor force, outright seizure and physical coercion were not unknown, and there was also some traffic in Indians. In conclusion, then, the methods used to coerce labor to produce and maintain the ranchos way of life was more extreme than European feudal relations. Class relations in California, as in New Mexico, were not limited to two classes—patrones and peones. Although in New Mexico, a middle strata of petty agriculturalists clung precariously to life, in California, the rancheros (*gente de razón*) were the patrones; the Indians hovered between peonage and slavery; and the Mexicans (and other mixed groups) occupied the middle strata. In effect, this meant that the Indian's unpaid labor served as the real basis of the economy; the Mexicans were the artisans, vaqueros, and foremen of the ranchos, as well as petty craftsmen in the scanty villages; whereas the *gente de razón* owned the means of production and occupied all the political and military positions. This situation, popularly depicted as idyllic, was far from utopia except for a few privileged families. The same social structure, at least in Southern California, continued for a few decades after the Treaty of Guadalupe-Hidalgo until it met its demise.

Before proceeding to an empirical and theoretical summary of the material basis of production and traditions in this area, brief mention must be made of Spanish colonization in present-day Arizona and Texas.

Arizona was settled as early as 1696, when Father Kino founded a number of missions including San Xavier del Bac, near present-day Tucson. By the end of his work, around 1712, twenty-five years of quiet was shattered by the discovery of silver in Arizona. After this brief silver boom, Arizona's economy came to be dominated by livestock production, insofar as the state was populated by the missions and some haciendas. However, from the middle of the eighteenth century onward, the area was the target of constant campaigns by warring Indians that made the maintenance of this frontier next to impossible. With the coming of Mexican independence and the disappearance of the defensive presidios, the area was abandoned and, from 1822 to 1862, suffered neglect and obscurity.[26] In the case of Texas, even though more definitive developments took place than in Arizona, its future course makes it more appropriate to be examined in a different essay.

The mode of production that developed and prevailed in most of Europe during the Middle Ages (feudalism) produced many of the forms that, with differences in location and time, the Spanish attempted to transplant in the New World. In many cases they succeeded. In a feudal mode of production the basic form of obtaining an economic surplus occurs through the appropriation of unpaid labor performed by serfs on the land. Whereas capitalism historically develops in and is based upon urban centers, feudal societies of production are based on the countryside. Since capital is mobile and ubiquitous, profit rates in different areas of production tend to become equalized; in contrast, land is immobile and fixed, and rents deriving from it tend to differ depending on fertility and other natural conditions. The study of the forms that ground rent took in Spain and Western Europe are important for an understanding of the developments that took place in northern New Spain.

Rent—in the form of labor services—was one of the oldest and most commonly practiced ways of securing agricultural surplus. It is probably correct to suggest that there is a chronology from labor rent, passing through rent-in-kind, to money rent. As far back as the fourth century B.C., the Chinese had learned to identify these three kinds of agricultural surplus. Whether labor rent is a more or less exploitable method than another form is also problematic. The Chinese philosopher Mencius considered labor services to be superior to others in that they provided the peasants subject to this service with the largest degree of stability, whereas the other two lent themselves more to the landowners' injudicious exactions, because the time required to work for the master was traditionally fixed and bore no relation to physical phenomena.[27] It provided the peasant ability to regulate the intensity of labor as the expectations of his master also varied. When labor services as agricultural rent emerged, the appearance of surplus paid in kind occurred, usually in the form of agricultural products, or in some cases, handicraft production.[28] It is not uncommon to find coexisting forms of labor rent and rent-in-kind, however. Money rent is characterized by the direct producer turning over part of a market product's price to the landowner. A surplus of products in their natural state ceased to be the norm, and the money-form took its place. Historically, the transition to money rent signified a step away from the earliest forms of feudalism toward the direction of a full-fledged monetary-market economy, though the latter is not necessarily a predominantly capitalist social formation.[29]

This is so because the feudal or capitalist character of a mode of production is determined by society's class relations or relations of production and not by the widespread existence of trade or money. If the existence of trade or money is considered the differentiating specification for capitalist development, the economic interpretation of history falls by the board, since we must assert that capitalism has always existed.

Also, within predominantly feudal European social formations, specific forms of land tenure concommitant with the direct exaction of ground rent by the upper class were common: typical examples are the proprietorship of small parcels; different forms of tenant-holding and sharecropping; and, in rare cases, independent owner-cultivators of medium-sized lots. Historically, these forms tended to disappear as feudalism gave way to capitalism. In the case of the proprietorship of small land-parcels, this was so because rural domestic crafts—a normal income supplement—were eventually destroyed by the development of large-scale industry, because methods of cultivation depleted the soil; because of the usurpation of common grazing lands; and because of competition—either from larger plantations or large-scale capitalist enterprises.[30]

The self-propelled estate where a peasant cultivator engaged in independent production was also bound to disappear: eventually he tended to become a small capitalist farmer exploiting the labor of others, or he lost his means of production and became a wage-laborer. Finally, with regard to the different forms of sharecropping, the crucial question is whether the relationship was, formally, a modern "business enterprise," or whether the substantive situation was otherwise, and the tenant holding arrangement merely a covert subterfuge for a more explicit form of rent-extraction.

Tenant-holding forms should *not* be confused with the case of independent capitalist cultivators who rent out the land and whose success is insured by social circumstance. Again, this is not to say that, on occasion, successful capitalist development cannot arise from the former. Whether any of these methods of sharecropping can lead to successful capitalist production is a rather determinable matter—statistically and historically.[31]

Of course, this kind of arrangement is suggestive of the possibility of breakdown of existing relations of production. This may be so because, although the tenant farmer may lack enough capital for self-sufficient management, the expropriation by the landlord goes beyond the old forms of rent, and interest on capital can appear. In other words, the direct producer or tenant, whether he simply utilizes his own labor or the labor of others, can now claim his income in his capacity as a capitalist rather than as a simple laborer. Conversely, the landlord can claim his share as a lender of capital as well as a landowner. Further, there was no dearth of this kind of economic arrangement in agricultural societies in their tributary state. A case in point is Spain where only slightly dissimilar forms appeared through the period of the *Reconquista*.

Spain was, of course, the source of the social institutions that were literally to find fertile ground in the soil of the New World. By the time of the Catholic kings, Spain had instituted the dramatically uneven distribution of income and wealth that was to develop so rapidly in New Spain. Despite the onset of commercial navigation, ownership of land and rents constituted the backbone of the Spanish economy. Spain, in its own particular way, was a society where commerce and capital were secondary to land ownership as the source of income and wealth.[32]

The basic feudal elements of medieval Europe and Spain were reproduced in New Spain. There is little to indicate that the developments that took place in the northern provinces were different from those that took place in the central valleys of Mexico. The hacienda system, with its patron-peon relationships developed later in New Mexico and California, but followed the same course as in Mexico and Spain. Purported differences between the California rancho and the New Mexico hacienda occur more in the way of nomenclature than in any significant matter. Of minor importance are, first, the rapidity with which the ranchos developed in California. But once it is explained that the groundwork had been laid by the more important role played by the missionaries in California, the speed of the transformation ceases to be a matter of concern. Second, the more intense racial overtones in California are due to empirically different circumstances. It is interesting to note that the colonization of Spain after the Reconquista shows a reverse trend. The first two centuries of colonization were characterized by a harsher relationship (outright expulsion and/or slaughter) toward the conquered Moors than those employed during the last few centuries of the colonization process. Otherwise, the basic mode of rent extraction was patently the same in California, New Mexico, Mexico, and Spain.

There are strong similarities—especially between California and New Mexico and the northern sector of Mexico—regarding the manner of colonization: expressly through subcontracting labor to political or military leaders of the Conquest, as well as through the rapid institution of large latifundias as the representative unit of social economy in the area. Again, there was nothing procedurally original in this process: rapid colonization by a few military leaders more or less anxious to settle the land among themselves typified the colonization of Andalusia in southern Spain during the thirteenth and fourteenth centuries.[33]

Perhaps one of the most popular misconceptions about New Mexico is the notion of presumed communalism. This misconception arises from the legal separation which existed between the land assigned to and independently cultivated by the individual peasant and the assurance of common water and grazing resources. In combination with the historical necessity to repel attacks from neighboring nomads, these factors presumably fulfilled the prerequisites of communal living. Communal organization for the purpose of defense cannot, in the long run, be viewed as substantial proof of a communal mode of production, anymore than footraces among communal people can be construed as evidence of competitive capitalism. These arguments are purely formal and do not advance any serious understanding of social change. Further, in the specific case of New Mexico, any communal preoccupation with defense was clearly secondary to the necessities of subsistence survival. This is clearly evident in the dispersal of colonial settlements and the dissolution of the towns—usually because the townspeople were more worried about being closer to their individual plots of land than to each other.[34]

Secondly, the existence of common lands disappeared in New Mexico, as it had earlier in Mexico, Spain, Poland, and Rumania, by a process of unswerving similarity. Private individuals (livestock owners in the cases of Spain, Mexico, and New Mexico) usurped the use of common lands until, eventually, free peasant proprietors were subjected to various forms of rent-exaction, while those who usurped the lands came to eventually control or acquire not only the communal lands but the lands of the peasants themselves. This was precisely the practice employed by the hacendados and rancheros. Of course, in some cases the legal protection extended to pueblos and settlements had positive results: in Spain, many towns were able to establish a measure of peasant independence during the Reconquista period; in Mexico, there were cases where the efforts of the townspeople in defending the integrity of the *ejidos* (communal lands) against the onslaught of the large landholders were successful. These efforts did not come to fruition in the northernmost settlements.

In my estimation, most of the confusion regarding this aspect of the history of the Southwest can be traced to its historians' concentration on three interrelated modes of interpretation: formal-cultural, legal, and institutional.

Formal-cultural interpretations generally focus on superficial or, in the final analysis, insufficient data to justify their claims. A common example of this approach is the description of inferior mental attitudes held by individual members of Spanish society. The "correct attitude"—as held by the historian—should embrace a certain willingness towards risk and uncertainty, since these facets are essential to the development of a business mentality. The opposite tendency—embodied in the notion of communalism—utilizes the same basis for argument: in both cases an explanatory structure is based on mental attitudes. Whether a business mentality or a communal disposition is preferred depends on the choice, or prejudice, of the individual historian. The failure to include the basis of *choice* between various subjective conceptions of what idyllic society is and was opens up a Pandora's box of relative choice. We enter a realm where the notion of historical progress is eliminated and one conception of the idea is as worthwhile as any other.

Other writers have been concerned with specifying the precise legal jurisdiction regulating the process of settlement in the area under study. Their activity cannot be condemned; on the contrary, it is a highly valuable task insofar as its practicioner does not fall into the error of regarding the letter of the law as the deciding factor of actual social relations during this period. Legal canons surrounding the issue of property in the land are important, not because they indicate that under the Spanish and Mexican governments every peasant was an independent cultivator, but because the study of subsequent developments reveals the manner in which laws were observed, i.e., where traditional practices supported by economic power prevailed over written legislation.

Of the three modes discussed, institutional history has perhaps been the most successful method used in identifying important structures in the history of the Southwest. This approach has specified the mission, the pueblo, and the presidio as the crucial institutions in the colonization of the Southwest. It is perfectly proper to speak of these institutions as the dominant instruments of conquest and initial settlement, but their discussion provides little understanding of the evolution of classes, the possibilities for and forms of economic surplus that originated in these societies and, finally, the directions for change which stem from this kind of social economy.[35]

The combination of cultural, institutional, and legal emphasis has implicitly produced a view of the Southwest as a peculiarly unique example of Spanish colonial society, sometimes referred to as the "Spanish borderlands."[36] My own interpretation is that nothing could be further from the truth. The basic socio-economic life of the northern provinces closely resembles the rest of Mexico and Latin America, and the same holds true—with slight variations—at the institutional level. There is no reason to believe that the land system of California and New Mexico would have had a future different from the process of latifundia and peasant exploitation that has characterized history south of the Bravo since 1848.

From this combination of historical and economic analysis, what are the main conclusions that can be drawn about the material substratum of life in New Mexico and California?

The strongest conclusion is the identification in both instances of a society which, in its process of development, resulted in a feudal form of social economy, characterized by a fairly rigid class structure and based upon possession and legal ownership of the land and by a separation in the distribution of this land. The coexistence of latifundias and minifundias and the predominance of the hacienda made this social economy indistinguishable from the rest of the Mexican social structure. By their nature, these aspects of the mode of production prevented the development of socially productive labor forces and the concentration of capital (though not of wealth) as well as the progressive application of technology in the agricultural sector.[37]

ii: Development of Commodity Circulation in the Southwest

Despite centuries of physical isolation, the old Southwest maintained an interesting array of trade ties with surrounding economies. Although the existence of trade has been popularly interpreted as a characteristic of "modern" societies, this is hardly the case, and such conceptions generally occur from viewing contemporary trade forms as the transactional norm. Trade between groups, clans, or societies has existed from the earliest times. It usually makes its first appearance as occasional exchange, and is linked to the extremes of scarcity or abundance in a primitive economy. Slightly more stable forms occur when surplus production becomes more or less consistent; silent barter, ceremonial gifts, etc., are stepping stones to and the initial manifestations of historical—rather than incidental—exchange.

The stage of "trade" proper, as it is commonly referred to, arises when the societies engaging in exchange are no longer self-sufficient; when trade is not reduced to a surplus which can be disposed of after the groups' needs have been fulfilled; when the surplus is no longer limited to a few specialized items since different societies have become specialized in production; when regional specialization forces the interdependence of adjacent groups; and when each group can no longer satisfy all of its own needs. In other words, trade in this form coincides with the appearance of markets and craft production.

In this form, trade necessitates the tradesman or merchant.

This individual makes his living by buying certain commodities at a price which is hopefully below their true value and selling them at a price which is hopefully above their true value. Consequently, trade develops and merchants thrive in conducting transactions between people living at different stages of productive development. People who enjoy the same level of economic development are less prone to enter into such unfavorable deals. As a general rule, trade is the result of uneven economic development and differences in productive ability.[1]

Before the Spanish *entrada* into New Mexico during the 1600s, trade had already taken place between earlier groups of regional settlers. In his first expedition, Coronado observed the existence of commerce between the Plains Indians and the Pueblos. The Plains Indians, skillful tanners of buffalo and deer hides, exchanged these goods on a regular basis for Pueblo corn, cloth, and pottery. Long-distance trade, so typical of the Old World at the time of the 1492 discovery, also existed in the New World during this period, primarily between the two major civilizations of the continent—the Aztecs of Mexico and the Incas of Peru. From Peru, a northward flow of metal and alloys—bronze, compounds of silver and gold, copper, gold, etc.—were exchanged for Aztec goods: precious stones such as amethysts, emeralds, and obsidians, weapons, dyes, embroidered clothing, and jewelry. In itself, trade was obviously not the product of Spanish influence on her new colonies.

However, Spain did impose trade regulations which became increasingly significant over time. In the case of Southwest settlement, as well as the rest of Spanish America, revolutions of independence marked a turning point in the development of commodity circulation or trade.[2] To understand this transition, we will explore the pattern of trade relations before 1821 in the specific case of the Southwest.

Beginning with New Mexico, it is possible to see at least three major aspects of trade affecting this frontier society. The first was the commerce that developed with surrounding groups of nomadic Indians. From the Comanches, Kiowas, and other groups, the New Mexicans obtained beef meat, tallow, and buffalo and deer hides, usually in exchange for knives, axes, muskets, liquor, and vegetables, especially corn. This trade relationship became quite organized, and traders from various New Mexican settlements congregated annually at the Taos fair where exchange took place. Additionally, numerous merchants from New Mexico ventured into Indian territory to engage in trade with the Kiowa and Comanche. Kiowa trade was conducted by a group called the *ciboleros*, or buffalo hunters (since these traders were also engaged in buffalo hunts as a part-time occupation). A more active intercourse developed with the Comanche, giving rise to the term Comanchero trade. This exchange involved, as it developed, a considerable amount of horse and cattle rustling at the Comanche end of the trade route in Texas. Trade with Indian nations became a vehicle for French-Spanish trade. French goods made their appearance in New Mexico in the mid-1700s. These commodities originated with the French in Louisiana, passed through the hands of the Pawnee Indians, and were then traded to the Comanche, who finally brought them to the Taos fair.[3]

The trade between New Mexican merchants was strictly regulated by Spanish authorities, who entertained their private policies of gift exchange and other forms designed to maintain good relations and peace on the frontier. A significant number of traders had no permission to engage in commerce, and the Spanish authorities did not encourage this trade.

The second aspect of trade in the Southwest settlement involved a commercial relationship with the rest of Mexico. The towns of New Mexico such as Santa Fe, were at the northern end of New Spain's network of communications: the Camino Real, or King's Highway. The Camino Real allowed the residents of New Mexico to maintain contact and receive subsistence supplies from the closest settlement on the road —Chihuahua, two hundred and fifty miles to the south.[4]

During the early period of settlement, Chihuahua became the center (and the Camino Real the avenue) of supply for the missionaries and other inhabitants of the northern provinces. A caravan service—similar to the long-distance caravans of antiquity—developed, at first, on an irregular basis from Mexico City to New Mexico. The trip occurred every three years and generally took six months in one-way transit. From Mexico City northward, the caravan carried mission supplies, missionaries, new settlers, baggage mail, and what was at first illegal private merchandise for exchange. During this early period, two forms of profit-making developed: one was based on the exchange of merchandise between different points on the route; the second was based on profiteering by caravan contractors involved in mission supply service. From New Mexico, a southward flow of local products initially included coarse dress fabrics, drapes, blankets, hides, and candles. As further trade developed, the northward supply of merchandise included boots, shoes, chocolate, sugar, liquors, paper, and ink. New Mexico was becoming a transactional center for the exchange of Indian and Spanish goods. By the mid-eighteenth century, an independent trade had developed between the merchants of Chihuahua and the New Mexicans, and an annual caravan moved between these two points. The times of arrival and departure from Santa Fe were arranged so that New Mexican merchants could visit the annual fair in Taos where trade with adjacent settlements took place. In terms of trade, the economy of New Mexico came to be monopolized by, and indebted to, the few Chihuahua merchants who had achieved a commercial monopoly through their receipt of royal licenses. The only other beneficiaries in New Mexico were large livestock owners who sometimes drove their own flocks of sheep to sale in the Chihuahua market under military protection.[5]

In addition, an active trade in slaves existed in New Mexico during most of the colonial period. Some traders engaged in this activity because it was far more profitable than trade in skins. It is also possible that some marginal settlers risked the dangers of reprisal to supplement their meager existence by hunting Indian men and women and exchanging them for various products. These slaves were usually traded to enemy Indian tribes or to wealthy Spaniards in the south who utilized them as servants and peons.

The case of California was somewhat different from New Mexico. The latter depended on the Indians for beef, tallow, and hides. On the other hand, California was self-sufficient in these items and used its surplus for export purposes.[6] Although California was settled by the Spanish toward the end of their domination of Spanish America (that is, during the most liberal period in trade regulations), a number of circumstances prevented the development of trade and outside communications. The overland south-north routes into California were desert routes, which effectively prevented the development of a well-trained path from mainland Mexico to California. California commerce during the colonial period can be reduced to a few items: hides and tallow exported to Mexico through the port of San Blas, and the provisioning of wine, flour, and grain to the occasional ships from other nations which put ashore in California. The latter were usually American ships engaged in the exchange of sea otter skins with a commercial house on the Chinese mainland. The California missions became far more prosperous than their New Mexican antecedents and did not have to depend on supply services as did the latter.[7]

In terms of colonial settlement, Texas had a more irregular history than either New Mexico or California. Texas was finally occupied during the 1720s, after a century of tentative colonization and retreat. Though sparsely populated throughout the colonial period, the impact of commerce and trade on the Texas settlement was perhaps more profound than in the previous cases. This was due, in part, to the size of the population involved and, more significantly, to the proximity of French settlements in Louisiana. Indeed, the geographical proximity of the French colony caused an active commercial exchange between the inhabitants of both areas. Although commercial intercourse was regulated by law, most trade was clandestine in character; smuggling enjoyed a high popularity during this period. The situation became accentuated after the Louisiana Purchase. As was the case in New Mexico, the supply services were managed by private merchants and government officials, usually for their personal gain. This official corruption generated a great deal of friction between state and Church authorities throughout the eighteenth century.[8] Although cattle multiplied with incredible speed on the Texas plains, livestock production did not become as integral a part of the social economy as had been the case in New Mexico and Spain. Smuggling, Indian slave trade, prostitution, and other such activities typical of border communities left an early imprint on Texas society. Despite its small population, the high degree of interaction with outside economies brought about the formation of an apparently complex society marked by a variety of "service" occupations (traders, interpreters, prostitutes, etc.).[9] Here, as in the nineteenth century, the history of Texas reads like a tabloid of adventure and exploit.

As a whole, the history of commodity circulation in the Southwest reflects Spain's colonial policy. Of course, all colonial powers sought to effectively control their trade with the colonies, but the degree to which Spain sought to regulate and appropriate the benefits of colonial possession was greater. Spain's colonial policy reflected the relative degree of backwardness into which she had fallen shortly after the discovery of America. Whereas in England and Holland commercial capitalists came to have an increasing influence in state trade policies, this was not the case in Spain. From the seventeenth century onward, England and Holland began to pursue a policy of "free trade" designated to benefit the domestic economic interests in ascendancy. The defeat of these interests in Spain during the sixteenth century left an absolute monarchy based primarily on landed interests who were occupied in colonial and world trade only insofar as their domestic position remained unthreatened. A typical policy of the Spanish crown was the institution in Sevilla of the Casa de Contratación (or House of Trade) in 1501. The Casa de Contratación had complete authority over commercial affairs with the colonies, and came to dominate commercial activities completely, since all colonial trade had to pass through the city of Sevilla. For many years, a ship could unload its cargo only at this port and a loading ship going to the colonies was required to pick up the goods at Sevilla. Although a change in ports from Sevilla to

Cádiz was effected later, all commerce still had to be transported by Spanish ships, and all colonial trade had to pass through a single town in Spain. Instead of placing trade in the hands of monopolies, the Spanish government attempted to effect a monopoly over trade.[10]

Trade regulations were as forbidding in the colonies themselves; neither foreigners nor their vessels could enter colonial ports, under penalty of death and loss of property. This trade regulation was added to manufacturing regulations which prohibited the production and cultivation of products that might endanger already existing production in the mother country.[11]

As we have noticed in the Southwest, these policies resulted in smuggling, a flourishing contraband trade, and the slow, grinding process of colonial development. Toward the end of Spanish rule, the Crown attempted to ease trade regulations. Certain cargo to the mother country could be carried to British vessels, and some trade was allowed among the colonies. These measures were prompted by the pressure of British interests and, in addition, by the imperative of colonial revitalization. Unfortunately, these measures were accompanied by a number of taxes and tariffs: Spain's renewed attempt to exact a maximum colonial profit. The remedy was too small and came too late. Napoleon's invasion of Spain coincided with the increasing discontent of a Creole class who wanted its share of the profits following other wars of independence in Spanish America. In Mexico, the alignment of the classes that ended Spanish domination was not as strongly dominated by commercial interests as it was in the rest of the colonies. This was partially because of the fear that a movement toward independence would become a social revolution from the bottom up (as Hidalgo and Morelos had hoped). Consequently, landed interests played a more important role in Mexico's independence. However, *the necessity to eliminate commercial restrictions became an objective element in the final dissolution of political ties with the Spanish empire.*[12]

The independence of the Latin American republics was immediately followed by the *elimination of trade restrictions, the rapid intensification of commerce, and the accessibility of Latin American nations to foreign commercial and industrial interests.* The pattern of economic and commercial development in the Southwest after 1821 reflected these trends which had occurred in the rest of Mexico and South America. The story has been told, not by the historians of South American trade, but in the diaries, legends, and even the folktales of the American West. One instance of this popular history is the entrance of the fur trappers into Mexican territory after 1821.

As early as the sixteenth century, Spanish explorers recognized the abundance and utility of furs in the area known as the Southwest. But since these explorers were mainly interested in the wealth to be obtained from gold and silver mining, large-scale ventures in fur trapping and trading really began with the American frontiersmen.

After the Louisiana Purchase of 1803, Spain began to use the fur trade as a diplomatic tool. By loosening the restrictions on trade in the area northwest of New Mexico, Spain was able to maintain Indian dependence through the exchange of pelts and other articles. In this manner, the Indians served as a buffer between the Spanish and American settlers, since the Spanish realized that the Indians had more to offer the Americans than they themselves did.

Southwest trade in the early 1800s generally consisted of coarse furs (buffalo and deer hides) and, for a number of reasons, did not develop further until the 1820s. High freight costs made the exportation of furs unprofitable; and, additionally, the warm climates of Spain and Mexico hardly accentuated their market value. Further, most Spanish colonists were too busy trying to subsist agriculturally to have much time for trapping. Of course, the main reason was that until 1821, Mexico was still owned by Spain. Before Mexican independence, a number of trading expeditions left the Missouri settlements for Santa Fe, but most were seized and imprisoned by the Spanish authorities. By enforcing severe penalties for trapping and the mere possession of furs, Spain hoped to promote and protect her own trade between central Mexico and the northern province.

During the first years of Mexican independence, Mexican officials were largely preoccupied with sustaining their power and developing their country. Consequently, no effort was made to enforce the old Spanish restrictions concerning fur trapping. Trade to the Santa Fe region developed rapidly, with Taos and Santa Fe as the centers for trapping and Indian trading operations. Merchants would bring goods to Santa Fe, and then return to Missouri with furs. In this way, the Santa Fe trade and the fur trade developed symbiotically.[13]

In 1824, the extensive trapping out of Taos and Santa Fe came to the attention of Mexican officials. Soon after, Americans were prohibited from trapping out of Mexican streams. Because of this prohibition, trappers began smuggling furs. Taos became a strategic location for traders: the streams of the Southwest were not easily navigable, thus overland transportation had to be relied upon. Because of Taos's remote location, furs could be taken out or supplies smuggled in without attracting the attention of Mexican authorities. Its proximity to the Santa Fe Trail was another asset. These qualities made Taos a perfect supply base for the overland route.

Since "foreigners" were prohibited from trapping beaver in Mexican territory, some men found it easier to become Mexican citizens than to risk smuggling penalties. Most of these men applied for a trapping license within one year of citizenship. They were also the men who gradually acquired vast amounts of land and contributed to the "bloodless conquest" of New Mexico by the United States.

The years between 1825 and 1833 are known as the Golden Era of Beaver Trapping. During this time, swarms of trappers operated out of Taos and Santa Fe, and the competition for beaver streams increased. There was a rapid expansion of trade between Missouri, Santa Fe, and Chihuahua, in addition to extensive traffic between New Mexico and California. "Trailblazing" to California, accredited to such famous "mountain men" as Jedediah Smith and Kit Carson, brought trappers into more promising beaver grounds and uncovered a convenient route to Pacific ports where furs could be marketed.[14]

Most of the beaver fur in North America was used in making men's hats. In the early 1830s, when silk began to be imported from China and, subsequently, more fashionable than fur, the price of beaver dropped. Although the decline in the price of beaver did not result in the decline of the fur trade, it did change the nature of the trade throughout the far West. After 1832, with the increased popularity of buffalo robes, the buffalo became the most sought-after animal. Unlike beaver pelts (which few Indians trapped), buffalo hides could be traded with the Indians. This meant that the fur trade could be carried out at trading posts and, in the mid-1830s, the stationary trading post became a dominant feature of the fur trade.

The impact of fashion, in concert with other factors such as the replacement of beaver with seal or rabbit fur, and the most obvious reason of all—the depletion of beaver streams cause by heavy unrestricted trapping—relegated the 1840s fur trade to the unimportant role it had played during the Spanish period. Once again, coarse furs dominated the trade and trapping became obsolete.[15]

Individual or small groups of trappers dominated the Southwest trade. In California, however, mountain men often held this occupation. Trapping in California was carried on by Hudson Bay Company, a large British firm which ran trapping expeditions throughout North America as well as Hawaii.

The early period of British fur trapping was characterized by poor relations between the Mexican government and the Company. No inquiries into Mexican land rights were made and the California government was so weak that Company officials held it in high contempt. No governmental protection was necessary since the wilderness in which the Company worked was far from any settlement, and the small number of beaver made trapping them impractical for the individual trapper. The Company attempted to extract the fur quickly in case there was an unreasonable border settlement. After 1838, the Company made an attempt to establish better relations with Alvarado's government. The Company was beginning to branch out into various agricultural areas, including cattle raising. Naturally, such an endeavor would be totally impossible under a hostile government.

By 1840, friendly relations had been established, but the agricultural plans never materialized, and California, which did not have a large beaver population to begin with, had lost almost all of its beavers.[16]

The colorful stories of mountain men roaming the West in search of fur occupy a significant role in American folklore. Often, however, these stories are not historically accurate. The available literature about the fur trade is rather poor. Writers seem overly concerned with legends rather than with the economic foundations of southwestern commerce. Research is inadequate in terms of the role of the fur merchant, the price of fur, the cost of other commodities, and the role of the American Indians.

In conclusion, the men who did the trapping should be mentioned. Although these mountain men have become historical heroes, responsible for opening an unsettled region to commodity circulation, in reality, they did not contribute to any significant change in the region's economy. They did explore, and caused the attendant destruction of resources, contributing to the alienation of the Indians. The trappers often remained in the area after 1840. Many became Mexican citizens, while others served as guides for the American government and for individuals going west. Their knowledge of the area's geography and the Indian tribes made them a valuable source of information to people who came later. However, the trappers were, first and foremost, men in search of a profit. While colorful, the lore which has grown up around them should take a backseat to economic considerations in social science research.

Equally important in the development of Southwest commodity circulation was the formation of the trade route known as the Santa Fe Trail. In 1821, William Becknell, traditionally known as the "Father of the Santa Fe Trail," took a trading expedition from Franklin, Missouri—a new river town—to Santa Fe. The route he followed was one of two commonly used routes, both of which crossed the plains to the

Big Bend of the Arkansas. From there, Becknell followed a tortuous mountain route over Raton Pass and across into New Mexico. Wagons could not, however, follow this route, and on his return trip Becknell bypassed the Raton Mountains and discovered a short cut across the Cimarron Desert, a flat, suitable area. On his trip, Becknell had carried his trade goods on pack animals and had reached Santa Fe by mid-December. Successful in selling out at a profit, he promptly returned home in January with news of the changed attitude of the authorities in New Mexico.

Encouraged by Becknell's reports, several expeditions left Missouri for Santa Fe in the spring of 1822. Becknell himself went along, taking three wagons—the first caravan ever hauled to Santa Fe and back—and established the Santa Fe Trail as a road. Although the caravan nearly proved disastrous (wagons had to go sixty miles without water), this cut-off proved more practical than the old one and other freighters soon began assembling in Franklin. Within a few years after Becknell's 1822 journey, annual caravans were traveling the nine hundred mile route from Independence, Missouri—the newly favored starting place—through dangerous Indian Territory to Santa Fe. Later, Council Grove—a city one thousand miles further west—became the starting point. The freight was transported in huge Conestoga-type vehicles, pulled by three or more yokes of oxen or teams of mules, and carried more than five thousand pounds of merchandise. These vehicles of early freighting trade came to be known as "Santa Fe trains." From the New Mexican bases of Santa Fe, Taos, and Albuquerque, beaver hunters could now exploit the area of the Southern Rockies. Thus, the widespread commerce of the prairies began. One of the most famous accounts of this commerce is the journal of a Santa Fe trader, Josiah Gregg. During eight expeditions across the Great Western Prairies, he recorded events and compiled them with his personal interpretations in a book. The first draft of *Commerce of the Prairies* was completed in 1843 and provides an eye-witness narrative history of Santa Fe during the 1830s.[17]

Traders had to contend with the burdens of travel, wagon

tools, official graft, and the attacks of Southwest Indian tribes. When Indian raids threatened the Trail, teamsters would travel closely together driving several wagons abreast. The caravans varied in size from year to year, but usually consisted of fifty wagons or less. At night, they would corral—or circle—and guards would be stationed. The rate of travel over the Santa Fe Trail averaged about fifteen miles a day and round trip passage usually took two to three months. Once in Santa Fe, the cargoes of textiles, lead, hardware, cutlery, glassware, and similar goods were traded for Mexican silver, mules, pelts and hides, blankets, and other items in demand on the East Coast.

When New Mexico became an American territory in 1848, traffic and trade over the Santa Fe Trail underwent many changes. For example, during the Mexican regime, the caravans made only one round trip each spring and summer; but with United States soldiers, civil servants, and settlers demanding goods, teaming operations to Santa Fe were modified to allow regular year-round schedules.

One of the largest wagon-freighting firms to cover the Great Plains was headed by three veterans of the Santa Fe Trail trade. Russell, Majors, and Waddell, a firm that grew wealthy from war rumors, became responsible for the movement of freight from Missouri to Salt Lake City, where a political rebellion threatened to occur in 1859. In transporting supplies for the troops ordered by President Buchanan, the firm established what became a standardized plan for the movement of men, animals, and vehicles. Although the firm eventually ended in financial ruin, it established a pattern for the march of wagon freight across the plains. In fact, the increase in freighting volume continued until completion of the various transcontinental railroads.[18]

The Santa Fe Trail, the lifeline of New Mexico, also served a military function after Cheyenne, Comanche, and Kiowa raids occurred in Colorado, New Mexico, and Texas. The Trail provided a route for military supplies to California and New Mexico volunteers with additional subsistence goods for the rest of the population. Many of these "Indian depredations" occurred along the New Mexico stretch of the Trail, where General James Carleton appointed an expedition under the command of Kit Carson to stop the Indian uprisings. This military endeavor—known as the Battle of Adobe Walls—led to a reduction of Indian raids on the wagon trains using the Trail and resulted in an 1864 treaty signed by the three tribes and the United States government: the Indians agreed not to engage in any further warfare either against settlements or against the traders of the Santa Fe Trail and to remain otherwise nonbelligerent. Although the Army continued to escort wagons on the Santa Fe Trail until the end of the war, there was little or no conflict with the various Indian nations along the route.[19]

The Santa Fe Trail was not an exclusive relationship between the frontier towns of Missouri and those of New Mexico. In fact, Santa Fe did not become the southern terminal of the Trail but simply a watering hole in the southern flow of merchandise. The old trail to Chihuahua now became the vehicle of continuation for American trade bound for all destinations south of New Mexico. From Santa Fe, American merchandise reached Chihuahua and Durango; trade links were even established with Sonora to the west. As such, these "local" transactions became part of the developing trade and influence of the United States with all of Mexico. However, the relative importance of this aspect of trade within the totality of Mexico's foreign commerce has not yet been determined. As American merchants moved farther into Mexico, they encountered constraints of commercial control and, consequently, a considerable amount of friction and contraband trade developed between Anglo tradesmen and Mexican officials in the northern sector.

In California, wealth took the form of live beef cattle and, as the period of independence from Spain commenced, this wealth entered into a lucrative trade arrangement with foreign vessels. Cattle were slaughtered for a small amount of dried beef for local consumption, and hides, tallow, and horn for commercial purposes. Money was scarce in California at this time, and almost all transactions were conducted by barter.

The value of hides fluctuated between one and three dollars, and the hides themselves were referred to as "California bank-notes."

In exchange for hides and other animal products, the *Californios* obtained a heterogeneous assortment of goods including liquor, cigars, sugar, spices, gunpowder, and furniture. Throughout the Mexican period, the hide and tallow trade provided the California rancheros with goods from the outside world and helped make California familiar in the East.[20]

Throughout the Southwest, all commercial activity had two major consequences. The first involved the utilization of a new trail between California and New Mexico that came to be called the Old Spanish Trail (although it had never been used by the Spaniards). These two provinces had never been in contact during the Spanish period and had remained in complete isolation from one another. The connecting path between these two settlements was originally established as a result of the fur expeditions from Santa Fe, when many trappers who came to California for pelts via rivers and streams found it easier to procure fresh mules and horses for the return trip.[21]

This mode of travel eventually developed into a lucrative two-way trade during the 1830s and 40s and brought blankets and other items to California in exchange for mules that would eventually find their way back to Missouri and beyond. Some of the same New Mexican traders who had previously engaged in slave and other trade with the Utah Indians became active on the Old Spanish Trail. Understandably, they were not welcomed by the placid landowners of Southern California, who treated them as they would any "foreigner." Trade on the Old Spanish Trail grew between 1830 and 1848, and disappeared rapidly thereafter.

The second major consequence of Southwest trading activity involved the development of communication routes reaching waves of colonists in the southwestern states. The importance of these colonists will be the subject of closer analysis in a later chapter, but one aspect of their migration is germane here. Just as the emergence of Santa Fe trade can be explained as a result of the pursuit of wider markets by American enterprises as well as in terms of Mexican independence, the appearance of colonists in the Southwest corresponds to the vagaries of American economic development.

By the time of Mexican independence, a large sector of United States economy could be identified as an internationally important center of industrial capitalism. Consequently, the United States began to suffer from those periodic crises which are the hallmark of a capitalist mode of production. What are now controlled recessions were previously known as depressions or, by yet another name, panics. Throughout most of the nineteenth century, two panics exerted considerable influence on the subsequent history of the Southwest. The economic collapse of 1819 gave tremendous impetus to the colonization schemes for Austin in Texas, and served to reinforce the flow of colonists migrating to Texas. Similarly, the crisis of 1837 was an important reason for the first flow of overland colonists to California.

In summary, what impact did independence from Spain and Mexico have on the economy of the Southwest in terms of trade development? As in any situation, the increase in commodity circulation carried an attendant disintegration of the simplicity of life that had existed before this time. But, as in every case, the appearance of commerce in a natural or subsistence economy had a disintegrating effect, limited by the nature of the producing community itself. In other words, whatever development or disintegration took place did so on the basis of the existing mode of production. This was certainly the case in New Mexico and California where the old class relations (which I have described in an earlier chapter) remained basically untouched. The traders, whatever their nationality, were regarded as foreign intruders within the traditional social fabric of these societies.

Secondly, as in the case of some localities in classical antiquity and in medieval Western Europe, the development of commerce in the Southwest was not conducive to the development of local industry and manufacturing, or to the growth of towns and handicraft industries. Commercial development only achieves these results under certain circumstances. The failure to do so is attributable to the fact that gains in long distance trade are often made not by simply exporting domestic products, but by promoting exchange between two or several backward, though unevenly developed, areas. In any given area, when less developed productive forces engage in commerce, there is a tendency toward monetary concentration in the hands of the merchants.

The development of commercial capital has been falsely associated with unremitting progress and the growth of urban centers. But these are empirical contingencies. Trade and commercial capital can also make their appearance among economically undeveloped, nomadic peoples—as evidenced by the Southwest before the Spanish invasion. In the case of the Southwest, manufacturing or industrial development did not occur as a direct result of increased commercial activity.

Neither commerce nor commercial capital should be confused with capitalism as a mode of production, since both commerce and commercial capital are much older than capitalism. The presence and development of commerce is an insufficient explanation of the transition from one mode of production to another. In fact, wherever merchant capital predominated in the history of capitalism in Western Europe, backward conditions and a stronger similarity to things past survived. It is fair to say that the development of merchant wealth has generally stood in inverse proportion to the general economic development of society. The history of Latin America is one large textbook example of this seeming paradox. Here, in twenty republics, a century and a half have passed during which the greatest accumulation of commercial wealth has been accompanied by the strengthening and persistence of social relations characteristic of the region before independence. The Latin American nations are all characterized as trading nations, as well as backward, semicolonial, and semifeudal nations. The monopolies that develop from the trade of backward societies have, at the basis of their existence, that very backwardness.[22] Insofar as this backwardness can be eliminated, the basis for trade exploitation will disappear and so will the monopolies arising therefrom.[23]

Wherever commercial capital has held sway, it has stood for all sorts of "illegal" enterprises, including robbery and piracy. In the case of the Southwest, the local expression of this aspect of commercial wealth was the excessive smuggling that developed, especially in Texas and New Mexico, after Mexican independence. Smuggling and contraband characterize the United States-Mexico border relations to this day.

In conclusion, the two most important and direct effects of the development of Southwest commodity circulation were, first, the unification of the area as one region and one market, especially as effected through trade on the Old Spanish Trail. Never before, despite legend and wishful thinking, had the areas of California and New Mexico constituted a materially unified area. This was done after independence in 1821, and was promoted by the spread of commerce in the western United States. Unification became an important precondition to the establishment of capitalism at a later date. Secondly, the trails opened by commodity circulation provided an avenue of escape for the newly dispossessed, those who sought relief from the crises of capitalist abundance. These colonists became the pivotal agents who would economically survive the political defeats of 1830 and 1848, and who would assist in the decisive implantation of a new mode of production in this old region.

iii: The Victory of Capitalism

How was the final defeat of feudalism in the Southwest achieved? What was the social significance of the Mexican-American War? The answers to these questions are both simple and complex: simple in that within a few years, a palpably different mode of the social organization of production predominated the economy of the Southwest; complex, in that with regional and chronological differences, a variety of social mechanisms and individual agents simultaneously influenced this change. In some areas, it is clear that economic forces—or differences in the methods governing the economic organization of production—were perhaps the most important determinants of social change; while in other areas (or at other times) purely economic factors are obscured, and legal (and/or extraeconomic forms of coercion) are clearly visible. As a whole, this situation is not surprising, if the process is one of social revolution: it is certainly more difficult to identify and to ascertain the impact of social forces in an epoch of upheaval and rapid flux than in an era of stability. This chapter will isolate the most significant elements effecting the transition from feudalism to capitalism in the Southwest. In doing so, a distinction will be made between economic and noneconomic processes and, at the same time, the economic aspect of basically noneconomic processes will be explored.

In reviewing the agents and agencies of historical change in the Southwest between 1821 and 1880, it is possible to identify four major contributors: the development of commodity circulation; the infiltration of independent colonists; the litigation over land titles; and the effects of usury capital. Since the development of commodity circulation has already been discussed, we will concentrate on the action of usury capital as the process that most clearly delineates the conflict between the two modes of production, recognizing that the importance of the remaining factors should not be dismissed.

Historically, the infiltration of colonists predates litigation over land titles and the development of usury capital by more than two decades, concurrent with the influx of traders after 1821.

In Texas, the era of American colonization began during the period 1819–21, when Moses Austin succeeded in obtaining (first from the Spanish crown and later from the Mexican government) the authorization to carry out a colonization project. The Panic of 1819 brought increased immigration to Austin's colony, and nursed a developing interest in other colonization projects.[1]

Between 1821 and 1836, the relationship between the American colonists in Texas and the authorities in Mexico City can best be recorded as a litany of vicissitudes. During this period, Mexico underwent what historians have referred to as the conflict between "federalists" and "centralists." In general, Mexican centralists encouraged the maintenance of colonial society; consequently, they derived their power from the landed aristocracy, the wealthy mine-owners, and the Church. They advocated a strong, centralized government under military rule, and tight control over local industry and commerce. The federalists formed the opposition and drew their members from the bourgeois classes. They represented independent commercial interests, incipient industrial enterprises, and advocated the elimination of Church privileges and the development of local autonomy in government.[2]

The Texas colonists were soon caught in the struggle between these two political forces. Many colonists entered Texas under the Colonization Act of 1824, enacted during one of the few periods when the federalists held governmental power. In addition, other colonists entered the territory under liberal contracts with the state authorities in Coahuila (the Mexican state that Texas was a territory of until 1836). After the federalists were defeated, the situation of various Mexican states deteriorated in terms of self-rule, and the future of those territories that hoped to become states became cloudy. By the early thirties, Mexico's colonial policy included firm military rule, the suspension of any promise of statehood, heavy duties on commerce, and restriction on further American migration into Texas.

Of course, most of what is now Texas had never been under effective Spanish control and other areas were, on the average, thinly populated. In Texas, American immigration had swollen the foreign population to more than fifteen thousand residents, and Americans vastly outnumbered the Mexican population. When the hostilities which eventually led to the independence of Texas began, the American residents had developed into a large settlement of self-employed colonists engaged in agriculture and commerce. Despite the presence of some slaveholders, the settlement was characterized by the absence of traditional bonds typical of Mexican society, and represented the transition to—if not the embryonic form of —an economy organized under capitalist modes of production. The settlement was certainly no longer characterized by feudalistic forms of land rent and peonage. But neither was it capitalistic, since the Americans were, with some exceptions, independent cultivators who did not employ wage labor in the manner of classical capitalist enterprise systems. Most importantly, the Texas settlement did not arise from the old society, but had grown side by side with it and independent of it. Consequently, its political independence from Mexico in 1836 was not incongruous with its history of independent self-development.

The War of Texas Independence did not set the territorial boundary with Mexico at the Rio Grande, but simply extended it to the Nueces River. Below the Nueces, the traditional way of life in the old Southwest, as explored in earlier chapters, remained uninterrupted until the war between Mexico and the

United States. In contrast, American settlers had clearly developed a different social economy. In summary, then, American colonists in Texas had not deposed the feudal system of the Southwest but, instead, acted as the harbingers of a new system which they implanted where the Spanish had not imposed theirs: the Texas settlement provides a case of erosion from without, not from within.[3]

Between 1836 and 1848, the section between the Rio Grande and the Nueces continued to be populated by Mexican immigrants. During this period, and for decades after the War of 1848, the lower Rio Grande Valley evidenced a system similar to the early California Settlement, with differences between various counties. After 1836, the role of the colonists diminished and other legal economic agents completed the economic transition.

In New Mexico, traders and colonists were virtually inseparable before 1848. A number of traders and fur trappers had acquired Mexican citizenship after 1821 in order to operate their businesses without the added restriction on foreign enterprise. In the later 1830s and 40s, some of these individuals were able to acquire landgrants from the Mexican government. However, these settlers cannot be categorized with the Texas colonists, since they identified themselves with the trend of large land acquisition occurring in New Mexico and California during this period. Former fur trappers and traders became land speculators and, as such, immediately affected the economic system of New Mexico. After facilitating the conquest of New Mexico by the United States, however, they continued their speculative ventures at the expense of Mexican property.[4]

California had a similar history in some respects. By the eve of the American occupation of California, Mexican and American residents had already acquired grants of the best land in the area. American landowners did not represent an immediate threat to the prevalent economic system then dominant in California, though some of them reinforced the rigid class structure of the state through marriage into important Mexican families and the further acquisition of landed wealth.

In general, a distinction should be made between American "farmers"—or those colonists who settled in Texas and became immediately antagonistic to the prevailing social economy —and American "landowners"—or those settlers who bene- fited from the existent order and did not welcome the erosion of land tenure systems.

With the exception of Texas, the Mexican Southwest underwent a unique pattern of historical development. The revolutionary power of a bourgeois state usually develops when the economic infrastructure has extensively modulated into a predominantly capitalist mode of production. In the South- west, the converse occurred: an American victory in the Mexi- can-American War ensured a succession of political and legal forms alien to the native economy of the Southwest. An impor- tant consequence of this development was the legal battle over land ownership following annexation. The origin of this con- flict began during 1820–48 and revolved around the manner of land distribution.

In California, some eight hundred grants of land were made to private individuals during this period. These grants collec- tively included over 8 million acres and were individually re- stricted to eleven square leagues. The availability of such large grants was facilitated by the secularization of mission lands and the last-minute rush for land titles before annexation.

The formal procedure for obtaining a landgrant began when the applicant filed a petition with the governor which included specific information on the individual and the land in question. The government then investigated the claim to en- sure the Mexican citizenship of the applicant or the availability of the land. If the findings of the investigation were positive, the governor would issue a personally signed document to the applicant as title to the land being granted. The grant was then surveyed and its boundaries marked. A record was kept in the governor's office of all petitions, grants, and maps of land granted. In many cases, however, the failure to comply faith- fully with the established procedure resulted in vague or over- lapping boundaries.

To obtain a landgrant from the Mexican government, the

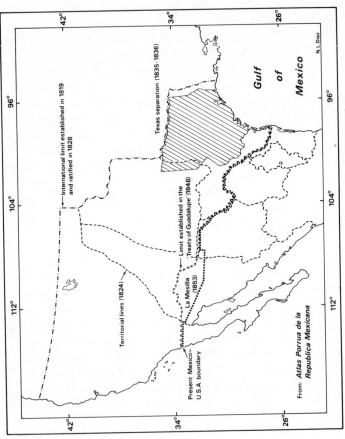

History of the United States–Mexico Boundary

International limit established in 1819
and ratified in 1828

Texas separation (1835–1836)

Territorial lines (1824)

Limit established in the
"Treaty of Guadalupe" (1848)

La Mesilla
(1853)

Present Mexico–
U.S.A. boundary

Gulf
of
Mexico

N.L. Diaz

From: *Atlas Porrua de la*
Republica Mexicana

applicant had to prove Mexican citizenship, although foreigners could receive grants if they were naturalized first. A map of the ranchos in existence at the time of the American conquest of California in 1846 indicates that one-eighth of the ranchos were located in the Sacramento and Upper San Joaquin River valleys and the majority were held by Anglos who had immigrated to California during the 1840s and become naturalized in order to qualify for ownership. Elsewhere, the rancheros were predominantly Spanish Californian. Several ranchos were held by christianized Indians who, under Mexican law, were considered citizens entitled to landowning privileges.[5]

Most of the land comprising the ranchos (that is, Mexican grants) lay in the southern part of California. In 1846, most of the northern territory was unoccupied and unclaimed by white individuals, as was most of the desert and mountain land throughout the state. Since ranchos rarely extended into the mountain regions, scarcely any of the area which irresistibly drew gold-seekers in 1848 was encompassed in rancho land.

Landgrant ownership was transferred in many ways and, certainly, on many occasions. Prior to the conquest of California by the United States, a grantee might lose his land if he failed to comply with the various terms on which he received it, such as the failure to occupy or cultivate the land. If an individual noticed this laxity and reported it to the Mexican authorities (at the same time making his own petition), and if governmental investigation upheld the secondary claim, then grant ownership was transferred to the second claimant.

The Treaty of Guadalupe-Hidalgo ceded California to the United States. Under the terms of this treaty, the United States pledged to respect all Mexican landgrants in California as the property of whoever owned them at that time. However, thousands of American settlers who came to California during the Gold Rush saw the best land tied up in ranchos; millions of acres of rancho land sat useless, land owned, but neither occupied nor cultivated. In their eyes, the rancheros were land monopolists and had no need of their vast holdings. Settlers like themselves, they reasoned, should be allowed to put some of this vacant land to better use. The Land Law of 1851 attempted to reach some resolution to the developing conflict between landowners and settlers. Under this law, a Land Commission was instituted to judge the validity of every claim to a landgrant brought before it. Any grants not brought before the Commission were automatically judged invalid and the area involved became public land open to American settlers.[6]

The Land Commission took several years to decide the validity or invalidity of landgrants. In the interim, a violent battle ensued between squatters and landholders in northern California. In most cases, the Land Commission's final decision favored the original claimant or grantee. By this time, however, the decision was essentially useless: if the original grantee had not lost his land to squatters, he had almost certainly lost it to the lawyers whose services he had engaged over several years while his case was pending, or else to moneylenders who had financed his litigation.[7]

Southern California remained basically unaffected by the change in government and land regulations. The influx of settlers during the Gold Rush was concentrated in the northern part of the state. There were two reasons for this development: southern California lacked the mineral wealth to attract miners; and southern California lacked good agricultural land to attract farmers, especially given the dearth of available water. As a result, land in southern California was generally devoted to cattle grazing.

In California, litigation over landgrants resulted in the ruin of many Mexican landowners, the spoliation of small Anglo-American settlers, the enrichment of some Mexican landowners, at the expense of others, but, most importantly, in the maintenance of large landholdings as the basic unit of California agriculture.

In concentrating on the failure of American law to recognize the property titles of its newly acquired citizens, some important details have been neglected. One point involves the nature of California's landholding class whose main interest and activity was the leisurely abuse of the Indian population. To defend the rights of California's landed aristocracy is as progressive as defending its direct descendant—the contemporary Latin American latifundio. The notorious racism of the vast majority of Anglo-American newcomers does not provide sufficient justification for the continued existence of an oppressive class as backward as the California rancheros. The tendency to do so constitutes a particularly one-sided example of nationalism.

Secondly, focusing on the losses incurred by landgrant litigation distracts attention from the original mode of acquisition where, under Mexican law, fraudulent, deceitful grants were chosen as the most effective assurance of aggrandizement in the transition from Mexican to American rule. The abuses suffered by new settlers under the Mexican landgrant system have also been ignored: many settlers were evicted—often through forged notices—from land which they had improved by its legal owner, who waited to claim it until it was improved. Thus, concentration on the vagaries of the litigation process has deterred attention from the final result of that process: *the maintenance of large landed property as a dominant element in California's economic landscape.*[8]

New Mexico provides a somewhat different case. In New Mexico, other methods besides litigation were employed to obtain ownership of the land. The imposition of American law made it difficult for some Mexicans to keep their land: the indigenous population, unfamiliar with the new landgrant statutes, could not easily defend themselves. The new land included a steep land tax which, because of the lack of a money economy, the Mexicans could not pay. The change to a currency-based system of trade extended an advantage to those who had a supply of capital—that is, to Americans with financial backing. Reclamation projects carried out by large companies also aided the transition by altering the ecology of the area: lowering the water level partially resulted in the demise of the small farmer. Finally, large tracts of land declared public were committed to the railroad companies or reserved as national forests. Consequently, the fight over land in New Mexico was not always peaceful; several conflagrations occurred, among them the Lincoln County War and the Colfax County War.[9]

The New Mexico experience both resembles and differs from California in this respect. Some large Mexican land-holders survived the early period of land title validation and, for a few years, became quite wealthy and powerful, especially through sheep-raising. Their eventual demise occurred through the onslaught of different forces. However, New Mexico's small agriculturalists suffered immediate harm under the impact of validation regulations and other measures mentioned above.

The Texas-Mexican experience with landgrant problems provides another variation: in some areas—such as Nueces County—large tracts which had been held by Mexican land-owners passed almost completely into American ownership by the time of the Civil War. Mexican landowners transferred their property under duress; many sold their land at a low price for fear it would eventually be confiscated. In Texas, more than anywhere else, the hostility between Anglo Americans and Mexicans had been long and heated; fraud, chicanery, and outright theft played a more significant role in the early transfer of land ownership from Mexican to American hands.[10]

Stressing the extraeconomic struggle over landed property in the Southwest deploys attention from a purely economic sphere, where the meeting of two systems of social production would eventually result in the victory of a capitalist mode. Even where Mexican landowners were immediately able to secure their holdings, they were eventually defeated. Validation and legal pressures were the products of an assault from without; the internal erosion proceeded at a slower, but firmer pace. If commercial capital had begun a process of disintegration, usury capital would deal the death blow to the old social formation of the Southwest. California and New Mexico both exemplify this process.

Prior to 1849, slaughtering cattle for their hides and skins sustained the economy of southern California. These were traded to Boston merchant vessels for manufactured goods produced on the East Coast. However, the population boom generated by the Gold Rush created a large market for beef in the northern counties. In 1849, California's Anglo population was only fifteen thousand; by 1852, it had soared past the quarter-million mark.

The ranchos quickly recognized this market for beef. In a letter to Abel Stearns, dated in the spring of 1849, Hugo Reid wrote from Monterey describing how the two could make a profit of twenty thousand dollars by shipping one thousand head of cattle from Los Angeles to the northern counties. Instead of transporting cattle by ship as Reid suggested, the ranchos drove them overland, up the coast, or through the San Joaquin Valley. The average herd numbered seven hundred to one thousand head, although herds of two thousand were not uncommon. Meat dealers' agents from San Francisco or Sacramento often traveled south to purchase cattle in Los Angeles, thereby releasing the ranchos from the somewhat risky business of driving the cattle north. Cattle sold for about seventy-five dollars a head in San Francisco, and thirty to forty dollars a head in Los Angeles. This was a considerable increase over the four dollars a head price in effect prior to 1849. The southern California "cow counties" were, in order of importance, Los Angeles, Santa Barbara, Monterey, San Bernardino, and San Luis Obispo counties. The most important of these counties, Los Angeles, was dubbed "Queen of the Counties" by the more prosperous northern cities. It was estimated that nearly thirty thousand head of cattle were annually sold out of Los Angeles during the seven year cattle boom.[11]

The cattle boom allowed the rancheros and their families to enjoy an opulent existence for a few years but, by the late 1850s and early 1860s, they were caught in a credit squeeze. During the bonanza years, many rancheros became indebted at high interest rates, expecting the boom to last indefinitely. Credit suddenly dried up, however, and the boom ended.

The lack of ready capital is a particularly interesting phenomenon. It would seem that the state should have been flowing with gold; but, in fact, most of the gold was shipped to the East to pay for goods purchased on credit in the interior. Most of the gold in circulation (ten and twenty dollar gold pieces) was coined privately along with the thirty dollar "slugs" issued by the assay office in San Francisco. Some examples of interest rates included:

1851   Juan Bandini borrowed $1000 at 4% per month.

1854   José Yorba mortgaged 17,000 acres of the Rancho Las Bolsas along with a vineyard for $5500 at 5% per month.

1854   Joaquín Ruiz borrowed $400 from Able Stearns for mortgage at 5% per month payable in one year.

1861   Julio Verdugo mortgaged his share of the Rancho San Rafael for $3445. In eight years the original debt had increased to $58,950, and he found himself a landless man.[12]

The demand for southern range stock began to fall as early as 1855 because of the influx of cattle from the Mississippi and Missouri valleys, and the importing of sheep from New Mexico. It is estimated that in the spring and summer of 1852, over ninety thousand head of cattle and twenty-five thousand sheep passed Fort Kearny en route to California. The following year, over sixty thousand head entered the state through major routes alone. During the late 1850s, the Midwest cattle drives greatly decreased, but this was offset by the influx of sheep from New Mexico, estimated to number one hundred thousand head during 1858 and 1859. The above factors caused a drop in the price of beef at the close of 1855. A bad drought in 1856 led many ranchos to sell their cattle at the lowest prices since the cattle boom began in 1849. By 1857, the cattle market in Los Angeles was completely glutted. According to a special federal census report in 1860, the more than 3 million cattle in the state were far beyond the "wants of consumption."

By 1860 all the ranchos were in serious financial difficulty because of delinquent property taxes, high interest rates, and the rancheros' financial ineptitude. Those rancheros who remained after a bad drought in 1860 and the flood which followed in the winter of 1861 were completely ruined by the infamous Great Drought of 1864. In 1860, grazing land in the area was assessed at twenty-five cents per acre; during and immediately after the Great Drought this assessment fell to ten cents per acre. The taxes of five-sixths of the property in Los Angeles County became delinquent in 1864. The great ranchos were sold to help pay off their owners' debts, mortgages, and delinquent taxes. Land syndicates usually purchased these large land holdings and subdivided them. The settlers who bought this subdivided land paid anywhere from $1.50 to $10 per acre.[13]

Was the demise of the California rancheros the result of a combination of purely fortuitous circumstances? In spite of any peculiarities exclusive to the region, what happened to southern California's rancho economy is not ·without precedent. When the development of exchange and monetary circulation has reached a certain level and a vast amount of social wealth is held in nonliquid amounts, usury and usury capital reaches its maximum development.

Historically, usury and commercial capital have appeared simultaneously with similar and slightly dissimilar effects. In different times and places, the development of trade and commercial capital has liberated the direct producer or the small agriculturalist from control by his lord or master as the development of exchange took place in a peasant economy. The reverse was also true: the development of exchange in the lord's economy intensified exactions from the peasants.[14]

In a similar fashion, the appearance of usury capital—where money is lent to the lord or landed aristocrat—can result in the impoverishment of the laborer or immediate agricultural producer. Usury has the added capacity to indiscriminately cause the impoverishment and destruction of rich landowners as well as the ruination of small peasant producers. In other words, "the usury which sucks dry the small producer goes hand in hand with the usury which sucks dry the rich owner of a large estate."[15] The pivotal power of the usurer in partially monetized economies rests in his ability to provide the means to pay taxes and other forms of monetary disbursement required of property owners.

Despite the popular conception of interest-bearing capital as the ultimate appearance of "capitalistic" social relations, it should be noted that money capital may or may not have a revolutionary effect on the old mode of production. It can and does disintegrate previous forms of production, although these paralyzed or crippled forms may survive for long periods of time. Only when other conditions are historically present can usury capital deal the final blow by ruining the landed aristocrat and transforming a small-scale producer into a wage laborer.

Returning to the California experience, it is evident that the demise of the rancheros at the hands of moneylenders is not an unprecedented, inexplicable phenomenon, but rather a well-precedented, theoretically comprehensible process. The complete and final defeat of the old mode of life was not, of course, accomplished by the influence of money capital. It was the sum total of a series of simultaneous developments—the struggle over land titles, high interest rates, competition with other producers, and natural catastrophes—which effected the transition.

Spanish and Mexican landowners were not the only victims of usurious interest rates; Yankee landholders who were old residents of southern California also had to sell their property in order to pay their debts. The influence of usury capital had an indiscriminate effect during this period. As economic theory would indicate, the wealth amassed by moneylenders was not qualitatively sufficient to effect a change in the mode of production. In fact, California lingered in a state of "under-development" for thirty years. Usury capital is not bent upon killing the goose that bears the golden eggs; it does, however, succeed in debilitating it.[16]

Some of the large landholders managed to alleviate their situation by leasing portions of land to gringo farmers willing to engage in capitalist agriculture. This method did not provide an effective remedy for the landowner's situation since general loan rates affected everyone equally forestalling capital intensive methods, immigration and, in the last analysis, capitalist farming. So, while usury capital did not ruin an existing class of small farmers, it restricted its ability to prosper.

In southern California, the late 1850s to the early 1880s were characterized by retarded economic growth.[17] As late as 1880, part of the original ranchos had survived taxes, mortgages, floods, and droughts only to disappear completely during the decade as a result of competition with other producers and the pressures of debts and mortgages. From the outset of the cattle boom, the ranchero cow counties had met competition from other producing areas able to undersell the southern Californians. These competitors included a number of Spanish and Anglo sheep raisers from New Mexico who drove their flocks through to the California markets. By the 1880s, California's traditional mode of life and production had been obliterated.

In New Mexico, the action of money capital is equally important, although the tempo and the focus of disintegration differs from California. As had been the case in California, the early period under Anglo-American occupation was favorable to the existing mode of economic organization. For almost thirty years after the conquest, Hispanic sheep owners were able to expand their territory into eastern Arizona, southern Colorado, and southwestern Texas. This movement was stopped by the economic competition and extraeconomic coercion of Anglo-American cattlemen converging on New Mexico.

Throughout this period and into the first year of the twentieth century, New Mexico's moneylenders applied a contained but firm pressure on Spanish landowners and American settlers alike. The demand for ready cash to meet a variety of obligations made many of the owners dependent upon the usurer's services. The ruinous effect of usury capital on landed wealth in New Mexico was not as visible as in California; in New Mexico, early recourse to litigation and fraud and, finally the war waged by Anglo-American cattlemen were empirically more decisive. However, the effect of usury capital on the poor can be clearly viewed in New Mexico as opposed to its relatively indistinct effect on California's dispossessed. The underclass of Old New Mexico—village dwellers and small peasants as well as the *partidarios*—continued to graze sheep on their small plots. As late as 1880, many partidarios survived in bondage to merchants and moneylenders instead of to their former patrones. With the advent of mechanized agriculture and the appearance of large-scale, commercially oriented sheep raising enterprises, those landholders who tenuously depended on moneylenders to stave off bankruptcy began to become wage laborers.[18]

Between 1880 and 1900, the area that had been annexed by the United States in 1848 had become predominantly capitalist. Whatever labor was utilized throughout the region was now wage labor, and accumulated wealth was acquired and utilized by capitalist investors in agriculture as well as in industry. This process was sealed by the development of rapid communication throughout the area advanced by railroad construction.

Although slavery was not an issue in the Southwest (1850 Compromise specifically avoided any reference to the issue), American settlers were very concerned with the Southwest's role in the Civil War. New Mexico remained loyal to the Union while Arizona joined the Confederacy. Significantly, the Mexican and Indian populations—those with no stake in the conflict—remained almost completely apolitical. After the Civil War, everything changed, when large investors became interested in the territories.

The corporations, as well as the individual Anglo settlers, considered Anglo-American ownership of the land an absolute necessity. In Arizona, this was accomplished through the Indian Wars. Unlike the New Mexico tribes, the Arizona Indians had been quite powerful, making it almost impossible for Mexicans or Anglo Americans to settle the territory. The Treaty of Guadalupe-Hidalgo did nothing to change this condition. By 1880, however, the reservation system was well underway, ensuring Anglo ownership of the land. After the confiscation of Indian lands in Arizona, large companies became the favored trustees. These companies made large-scale attempts at irrigation, and their success resulted in larger profits, particularly after the railroads opened up eastern markets. Until 1896 when the government also began irrigation projects, only large companies could farm profitably. The growth of agri-business had begun.

In New Mexico, the coming of the railroads also encouraged the growing of crops for eastern markets. This farming did not match Arizona's scale, however, as irrigation was limited. Furthermore, cattle ranchers exerted greater control over the land and opposed the spread of large-scale farming.

The cattle industry had been based on the "open range" concept—that is, ranching on public land. Huge profits were made in this industry, particularly during the Gold Rush, when beef was in heavy demand. In the 1880s, a combination of factors caused the end of the open range cattle industry in New Mexico and Arizona. The 1886 blizzards killed large numbers of cattle, and the invention of barbed wire allowed owners to pen their cattle, thus making it more profitable to own land than to keep it in the public domain.

The cattle industry did not constitute the first ranching enterprise in New Mexico. Until the end of the Civil War, sheep farming was an extremely profitable venture for some members of the Mexican population. Between 1852 and 1858—the years of the Gold Rush—over five hundred thousand sheep were driven to California. After the Civil War, however, California developed a surplus which drastically cut profits. Wool remained an important source of income until the 1890s, when the onslaught of drought, the removal of tariff protection and the Panic of 1893 destroyed the industry.

The growth of the cattle industry had some significant results. It caused a great deal of animosity between Mexican and Anglo communities as sheep herders and cattle ranchers fought for control of the land. Besides this negative effect, however, the industry positively benefitted both territories. It was in part responsible for the great population growth of the 1870s and 1880s because as the cattle industry produced astronomical profits in Texas, real estate companies began to "sell" people on New Mexico. Coupled with the coming of the railroad, the population rose by twenty-five thousand in New Mexico during this period (an increase of 20-25 percent). Cattle and sheep industries also generated a large flow of capital into the area, accelerated by the railroad's guarantee of easy access to eastern markets. The growth of these industries was significant to territorial development during this era.[19]

The mining industry also played a role in the development of the Southwest. In New Mexico, this industry was not as important as in Arizona. After the Civil War, gold was discovered and produced much wealth in 1867 and 1868. In the ensuing years, however, silver played a much more important role, but in 1893 the silver market crashed and destroyed the industry. Copper mining, which was to play a significant role in the history of the state, did not get started until the twentieth century.

Arizona had a much large number of mines, particularly those owned by concentrated economic interests. The demand for labor caused a population boom in the mining towns, particularly after the advent of the railroad. Gold and silver were the major metals mined until the Panic of 1893. As in New Mexico, copper mining did not commence until the twentieth century. Significantly, large corporations played a more important role in the development of mining in Arizona because they had a larger influence than the small-scale operations of New Mexico.[20]

As discussed earlier, the Southwest's rapid growth was, to a great extent, caused by the railroads. Throughout the area, there was a pressing need for cheap freight transportation and, by the end of the 1870s, railroads were established. (Earlier attempts had been destroyed by the Panic of 1873.) Since handsome profits could be made constructing railroads, the rush to build them resulted in a surplus distinctive to many of the smaller railroad companies, adding to the growth of centralized capitalistic enterprises.

The railroads assumed monumental importance in ending the age-old isolation of the West. They opened up eastern markets to southwestern products and facilitated the import of heavy machinery used in mining. Other equally important capitalist developments took place in California and Texas during these years, but they properly belong in a separate chapter.

The geographic border of 1848 disappeared during the Mexican-American War and a new border was delineated. In economic and social terms, the border still existed north of the new juridical line, and this period witnessed the elimination of former economic and social distinctions prevalent in the area. Meanwhile, beginning in 1848, the area immediately adjacent to the border line became the center of economic conflict with the Mexican Republic, but this too is a subject for a later chapter.

iv: Establishment of a New Border

With the signing of the Treaty of Guadalupe-Hidalgo, a new border existed between the United States and Mexico. It took a few years to complete the work of surveying the boundary and, consequently, except for that portion traced by the course of the Rio Grande, the separating line was not defined for some time. A few years after 1848, the border lying between the Rio Grande and Colorado River was redefined. The Gadsden Treaty—as the purchase of this additional territory was called—was negotiated to obtain a convenient railroad route to the Pacific Coast as well as to obtain mineral rights to the area.[1]

For a number of years, the border line consisted of two major sections which met on the Rio Grande above El Paso: the line drawn from the Pacific Ocean to the Rio Grande, and the course of the river itself. Of the two, the former could not be geographically identified as an international boundary. The only settlements in existence at the time, and for a few years later, were on the Rio Grande. In 1853, only the States of Tamaulipas and Chihuahua had towns on the border with the United States. The population of these settlements was thin and almost nonexistent along the rest of the border. Many Indian groups displaced by the United States Army roamed over this unsettled area.[2]

Because of the lack of basic research on the border area during the second half of the nineteenth century, it is somewhat difficult to identify more than a few basic structures and events which played an important role in the socio-economic transformation of the region. To introduce the student of socio-economic transformations to three major focuses, it is necessary to isolate those themes which concurrently emerge from 1830 to 1910 in this northern area of Mexico. The first theme concerns the isolation in which the northern area of Mexico continued to survive thirty years after the Treaty of Guadalupe-Hidalgo. Based on the lack of efficient transportation, and affected by such momentous events as the French occupation of Mexico, the isolation of the northern area prevented any effective connection with the national economy as well as inhibited the task of frontier defense. At the same time, the economic control of production by large latifundista cattle raisers remained unchecked.[3]

Secondly, whatever the objective needs of the economic system and/or the subjective whims of its officials, the United States continued to entertain the idea of further occupation of Mexican territory.

Thirdly, though the period from 1848 to 1914 is known as one of world peace, it is precisely during this period that the newly formed border between the United States and Mexico became a bloody arena of cultural, racial, economic, political, and military conflict. For the borderlands, these years were characterized by chaos and turbulence.

Evidently, these three themes are separable only heuristically, and the same is true for the division of conflict into political, economic, and social spheres. The border area appeared as a result of the clash between two economic systems—a clash which eventually ended in military confrontation, expropriation, and social chaos. It would be the height of naiveté to believe that peace and calm could have ensued in the wake of such historical developments. The struggle that characterized the area can only be isolated for the purposes of clarification, understanding, and explanation.

The creation and development of the so-called Zona Libre provides a specific instance of the themes sketched above. For almost fifty years, beginning shortly after the Mexican-American War, a strip of territory along the northern part of Mexico known as the Zona Libre played an important role in the economic and political relations between the two countries. At the height of this development, the Free Zone extended for 1,833 miles from the Gulf of Mexico to the Pacific Coast and was 12.5 miles in width. The importance of the zone was based on tariff differentials which could be enjoyed within the zone. Although the zone was never completely free of tariffs, the differentials were large enough to provoke a great deal of national and international anguish and conflict.[4]

Shortly after the signing of the Treaty of Guadalupe-Hidalgo, a peculiar situation developed among the towns situated on both banks of the Rio Grande in that radically different prices prevailed on the two sides of the river. The usual explanation given for this development is that in the United States no taxes or restrictions of any kind were levied against internal trade, and there were minimal taxes on foreign goods. In contrast, on the opposite bank, the "old system" prevailed—setting heavy taxes on foreign goods while a variety of levies against internal trade led to a restricted domestic commerce. There were also heavy protectionist restrictions in Mexico on the number of commodities which could enter the country. As a result of this situation, different prices existed on each side of the border. On the Mexican side, higher prices were charged for goods of domestic production and consumption, and an even higher price was laid on foreign goods than on the American side. As a consequence of this disparity, people were either leaving Mexican towns and settling on the American side of the river or were actively engaged in smuggling goods across the border into Mexico. At the outset, two sets of commodities were involved in the controversy. One set involved locally (Mexican) produced provisions essential to the population, whose apparent dearness forced migration to the left side of the river; the second set consisted of foreign goods. The controversy surrounding the latter has never been made entirely clear. Arguments over the causes and consequences of the Free Zone are so tangled with political interest that it is imperative to begin any discussion by making careful distinctions between these different aspects of the problem.[5]

The situation of forced migration across the river to the United States developed quite early, and it became grave enough to force the central government of Mexico to authorize the importation of provisions through the border customhouses of Tamaulipas at reduced rates. This permit severely limited the flow of other goods—namely, those produced far away from the border, either on American's eastern seaboard or in foreign countries. The next crucial step was taken by the United States. In 1852, the United States passed an act by which foreign goods imported into the United States could be sent in bond to Mexico over certain specified routes. These goods could be held indefinitely in warehouses on the border and, if sent to Mexico, were exempt from export duties.

This move made the situation on the Mexican side of the river far more precarious. In relative terms, it also indicated that commercial houses on both sides of the border placed a greater importance on the prices of foreign goods than on locally manufactured provisions. Evidently businessmen involved in European imports and located on the left bank could exercise commercial predominance under the new act; they could smuggle European commodities into Mexico at a very low price, thereby ruining Mexican merchants as well as influencing English and other European sales in the area.

Out of this situation the Free Zone emerged. It was not only a response to the actions of the United States and to the prevalent practice of smuggling, but issued from the desire to strengthen the border settlement. To some extent, the Free Zone also served as a battleground for American and British commercial interests. At the state level, the forerunner of the Mexican Free Zone was established by the governor of Tamaulipas in 1858. For all intents and purposes, he established by decree what came to be known as the Free Zone. All foreign goods used in the frontier towns were exempted from federal though not from state and local taxes. The decree also allowed "in bond" warehouses in border towns. The struggle was obviously one between dealers in foreign goods on both sides of the river: British goods imported through ports at the mouth of the Rio Grande could sell more cheaply than the same goods that, having arrived at U.S. eastern seaports, had to be transported halfway across the United States. More importantly, European goods in the Mexican towns provided a spirited competition to many American manufacturers.

The institution of the Free Zone in Tamaulipas was intended to reverse the flow of smuggling towards the United States. Additionally, since tariff duties were not lifted outside the Republic, the Free Zone provoked a considerable amount of smuggling back into Mexico. The Tamaulipas legislation was confirmed and enacted into federal law in 1861. From then on, in the eyes of American officials, the existence of the Free Zone was intimately connected with smuggling, banditry, border violence, and hostility on the part of Mexico. Within Mexico, there was some opposition to the establishment of the zone, stemming mainly from interstate rivalries. It was the feeling of at least some important cabinet officers that the establishment of the Free Zone amounted to playing provincial favorites and caused undue damage to commercial interests in other states. These views never held much sway in Mexico, especially since many nationalistic officials viewed their coincidence with American interests as ample justification for dismissal.

A few years later, the Free Zone was extended to include the additional states of Coahuila, Chihuahua, and Sonora as well as the territory of Lower California. By the 1890s, the economic impact of tariff liberality in this area caused a decreased tariff differential. Secondly, new regulations such as the 1891 statute regulating import duties on commodities manufactured in the zone and coming into the rest of Mexico—whether of domestic or foreign raw materials—provided an impediment to the development of manufacturing interests inside the Free Zone.

The direct effects of the Free Zone were also influenced by changes in the relative productive power of the United States and other industrial countries, as well as by such historical events as the American Civil War. The impact of the latter was later confused with events caused directly by the existence of the Free Zone itself. Briefly, the outbreak of war in the United

States made the existence of free and neutral ports of paramount importance. The cotton trade, contraband war materials, and supplies of various kinds began to flow through Matamoros. Within three years, Matamoros had become one of the busiest *international* trading centers, with up to eighty ships anchored in its harbor at any given time. Between 1861 and 1865, the population of Matamoros grew from less than five thousand to almost forty thousand residents. Once the war was over, the trade in weapons and cotton declined rapidly, as did the wealth and business of the town. Within a decade, it barely counted five thousand residents.

The Free Zone was established with the purpose of alleviating the flight of Mexican citizens across the border. Some of its side effects were disastrous. The considerable smuggling into Mexico caused the consequent loss of treasury revenues and provoked some smuggling into the United States and the attendant protest of the American government. The existence of the Free Zone was one of the many factors causing serious friction between the United States and Mexico during this period. The controversy involved American nonrecognition of the Díaz government for almost two years and, in the 1870s, it became the central issue in all relations between the United States and Mexico. The United States viewed the existence of this Free Zone as an unfriendly act and, for some years, applied diplomatic pressure to have it removed. Beginning in 1870, the president's annual State of the Union address mentioned the evil nature of the zone as a base for smuggling across the boundary into American territory. The American press and governmental officials also connected the existence of the zone with the violence and depredations of Indians and cattle rustlers.[6]

A Mexican Border Commission instituted to investigate the situation in 1873 indicated that Americans, in making complaints of Mexican raids and the Free Zone, were seeking a pretext for annexation of Mexican frontier territory. This was not, by any means, an intemperate accusation. In the specific case of the Free Zone, its original purpose became reversed over time. By the mid-1870s, the decline in the price of American manufactured goods, coupled with the development of the railroads, had enabled American merchants on the Texas side of the river to successfully compete with Mexican merchants who dealt in European products. From being a barrier to the predominance of American imports, the Free Zone became a haven for those American manufacturers who were the sole beneficiaries of the liberal tariffs on foreign goods. Not only did American commercial capitalism dominate the area, but restrictions on manufacturing prevented the independent development of the area. Despite this reverse in the function of the Free Zone—which in fact had become detrimental to the best interests of Mexico—the government of the United States continued to use the Free Zone as an excuse for continuous harassment, threats of invasion, and military incursions into Mexico.

Before the Free Zone was established, the border area had been tormented by violence. The area between the Nueces River and Rio Bravo may be characterized as a no-man's land ravaged by guerrilla warfare and battles between Texas and Mexican regulars during 1835–48. The immediate causes of violence are interwoven in a variety of ways; in this area, racial tensions, the "lawlessness of the frontier," international questions, and the "economic battle" simultaneously occurred. For example, warring factions involved Texans against Mexicans, Texans against Texans, and Mexicans against Mexicans. One net result of this violence involved the partial rout of Spanish landowners seeking refuge in the towns.

Before the American Civil War, a number of major outbreaks had occurred and a continuous state of violence prevailed along the Rio Grande. Historians have referred to the first major outbreak as the Merchants' War.[7] The direct cause of this incident was closely related to the tariff issue. Before the Treaty of Guadalupe-Hidalgo became effective, American merchants had managed to introduce large quantities of their commodities into Mexico. Under the conditions of the treaty, no tariffs were to be levied against any of this merchandise. Mexican officials proceeded to levy some duties upon certain goods transferred from American warehouses at the signing of the treaty, and whenever payment was refused, they confiscated the merchandise. Quite a few incidents of this nature took place, naturally infuriating many American merchants who saw British interests behind the tariff situation. Their collective response was to organize the first "filibustering" band, led by a Mexican adventurer under the guise of creating an independent nation—certainly one without tariffs on American goods—out of the northern Mexican states. Prompted to launch the adventure, not only because of restrictive tariffs, but also because their first response—smuggling—had been stopped with unusual vigor by Mexican authorities, their several expeditionary excursions into Mexican border towns met with unremitting failure. More than anything else, the Merchants' War is important because it took place at a time when other "adventurers" were launching filibustering expeditions against Central America, Cuba, and other sections of Mexico. Secondly, from this date forward, the increase of expansionist filibustering in the area reached such proportions as to merit Rippy's characterization of the period up to 1878 as the "Golden Age of Filibustering."

A second source of friction concerned the activities of Indian "depredators." In reality, this classification is a misnomer: many raiding parties were composed of Mexicans, Negroes, and whites as well as Indians. The reason for "Indian" violence was, once again, connected with the fact that Indian groups were being as economically and culturally dislodged as the Spaniards and Mexicans. The Indians in these marauding groups were usually members of wandering "nations" seeking refuge in Mexico after they had been forced from the hunting grounds and fertile soil of lower Texas to the barren plains of Chihuahua and Sonora. It is hardly surprising that they were driven to violence and depredations. Under the excuse of punishing the raiders, however, parties of Texans repeatedly invaded Mexican territories, meeting reciprocal action by Mexican army chiefs. Another incident of violent attacks by army troops and armed civilians on both sides of the border occurred over the flight of slaves into Mexico (and probably the flight of peons into the United States). The pursuit of these fugitives led to numerous American raids into Mexico.

With the onset of the American Civil War, the attention of the United States ceased to focus directly on the border, and Mexican towns were able to prosper, partly because of the war and partly because of the Free Zone. After the war, however, American attention became refocused on the border.

As I have already mentioned, the American government viewed the Free Zone as a source of smuggling into the United States, and interpreted its establishment as an act of hostility by the Mexican Republic. In the 1860s and 1870s, when border raids and frontier agitation had become more frequent, the Free Zone became a center of controversy. Public denunciation and the "desire to pacify the frontier" were offered as the basis for America's nonrecognition of the Díaz government for almost two years.[8]

The Mexican response to these accusations was cool and perceptive. The 1873 Mexican Commission report indicated that claims of American losses were exaggerated and raids by Texas bandits were as much to blame as raids by Mexican bands. The issue exploded with the development of the "hot pursuit" strategy favored by generals as ample justification for the complete eradication of bandits and marauders from the border zone. In his memoirs, the ambassador to Mexico at that time (Foster) indicated that the practice might be explained as a plan to use pressure upon the Mexican government in order to present the alternatives of hostility or sale of the northern states of Mexico. Whatever its ultimate purpose, the appearance and development of banditry plagued the border area through at least fifty years of violence.

For a variety of reasons, between 1850 and 1900, the border area was a fertile ground for the development of banditry. Social scientists who have delved into the myths and legends surrounding this phenomenon have unearthed a number of factors and circumstances usually contingent upon the appearance of this social practice. The first prerequisite for banditry is proximity to a major geographical or political border, preferably the latter. The ideal situation for a *bandolero* is one where he can operate in a particular location and use another for refuge from legal extradition. There is also a close correlation between the appearance of banditry and the onset of a period marked by pauperization and economic crisis. Since the practice in question occurs, in our discussion, in rural, peasant areas, the expropriation of peasant lands provides ready evidence of pauperization. In this respect, a period of economic crises can result as a consequence of "surplus" rural population, due either to the expropriation of property or massive migration. As opposed to overpopulation, the concept refers to the existence of landless groups of individuals.[9]

During several decades of the nineteenth century, all of these factors were present along the United States-Mexico border. The border's proximity and the rough terrain surrounding it provided bandits on both sides of the border refuge and easy escape routes. Pauperization characterized several cultural groups inhabiting the area in the immediate vicinity of the Rio Grande and was especially true of many Indian groups in the area. In concert with the Indians and other dispossessed peoples (runaway black slaves, marginal white colonists), Mexican settlers who had either lost their land or been forced to abandon it created the "surplus" rural population which spawned the bandolero. This development occurred in California as well as in Texas, although, given the distance of California banditry to the California border, it is less important to our analysis.

The growth of banditry in the area was also caused by the coincidence of several forms of economic and social oppression. In Mexico, since most of the land was owned by large haciendas, the absence of settlement incentives inadvertently supported the border's "surplus" population and did nothing to mitigate the presence of bandits, cattle thieves, and other criminals. In the border area itself, American citizens fought with Mexican citizens; Indians fought against both; the rich were set against the poor; and governments on both sides of the border had to deal with their respective and collective tradition of criminality. With the advance of the railroads and the further penetration and establishment of industry below the border, the intensity of violence subsided.

During the construction of its transportation empires in the Southwest, the Pacific Railroad projects—the Kansas Pacific, the Atchison, Topeka, and Santa Fe, the Southern Pacific, and the Texas Pacific—received huge grants of public lands. Between 1850 and 1871, more than 150 million acres of public land were given to western railroads. In granting these large sections of land to the railroad corporations, the federal government took land from the public domain; former settlers suffered great losses of land in New Mexico and Arizona; and the incursion of people and commerce brought clashes of violence and destroyed the old ways.

During the 1870s, the United States began importing Chinese workers and exploiting their labor in railroad construction. Many thought that the Chinese could become a major labor force, but anti-Asian bigotry caused Americans to begin excluding them.[10] Although railroad companies like the Southern Pacific were more concerned with the financial advantage of Chinese laborers, immigration legislation totally excluded the Chinese after 1884. Railroad managers then turned to Mexicans as the next cheapest source of labor for railroad crews. When the demand for Mexican labor could no longer be supplied by Sonora alone, the United States recruited further into Mexico. The increased area covered by Mexican railroads made the importation of Mexican workers easier.

Mexico itself began railroad construction very slowly. During the Juárez administration (1867–72), the British were authorized to build a railroad between Veracruz and the capital. The program failed, however, because the rails laid with foreign money and skills were built to support foreign capitalists rather than to enhance national economic development. The rail lines grew in patchwork formation and were never designed as strategic national transportation networks.

When Juárez died in 1872, Sebastián Lerdo succeeded him to the presidency. Lerdo continued the policies of his predecessor, but refused to allow railroads to be built toward the north or to connect with North American tracks beyond the border, since connecting the two lines could give the Americans a military advantage. In America, powerful railroad interests were angered and Lerdo had to fight for reelection, which he won but did not maintain. Porfirio Díaz took advantage of the politically unstable situation in Mexico and was finally declared president. The base of Díaz's economic program was railroad construction; economically, railroad building and industrialization were the two most important innovative processes generating social change in Mexico during the Porfiriato.

Prior to Díaz's seizure of power, only four hundred miles of track had been laid. During his administration, the federal government began selling huge tracts of Mexican soil to foreign companies and native hacendados. In the northern states, railroad concessions were sold to the United States. Within three years after the Díaz recognition, concessions to America provided for the construction of five railroads in Mexico aggregating over twenty-five hundred miles and carrying subsidies of over $32 million. These lines went from north to south and provided a route to the interior of Mexico from which ore was transported to the United States. The Southern Pacific had been extended eastward as far as Yuma, Arizona, in 1877 and in 1881 was extended to Deming, New Mexico, and El Paso, Texas, connecting at Deming with the Atchison, Topeka, and Santa Fe. Other major railroads linked routes through the southwest region and, at the same time, work progressed rapidly south of the border. The Mexican Congress granted concessions with the stipulation that the roadbed would revert to Mexico at the end of ninety-nine years. Díaz kept his promises, believing at this time that North America would otherwise forcibly seize the railroad concessions.

Between 1880 and 1910, American and other foreign capital had financed the building of fifteen thousand miles of track. As communication and transport improved, the degree of lawlessness and banditry began to subside, although it did not altogether disappear. One of the more curious episodes in the long campaign of pressure and threats, which typified the conduct of the United States towards Mexico before Díaz, involved the roles played in the negotiation of railroad contracts by one Mariano Vallejo—a California farmer—and General Frisbie—Vallejo's son-in-law. The two acted as semi-official agents of the United States to the Mexican government; their plan was to force Mexico to sell some of its northern territories under threat of armed attack by the United States.[11]

In summary, the violence of this period was promoted by and affected both sides of the border. The United States utilized the issues of violence, cattle rustling, "Indian" raids, and the Free Zone, regardless of their inaccuracy, to successfully apply enormous pressure on the Mexican Republic in order to facilitate the growth of American investment enterprises in Mexico. In some cases, border "violence" can be recorded as ruthless economic competition. Much of the "cattle rustling" that occurred in the area usually referred to the practices of large Texas cattle owners who would launch "expeditions" against similar Mexican entrepreneurs south of the border. The amount of cattle rustling quickly diminished as the grazing property of northern Mexico passed into American ownership.

The railroads developed concurrently with the tremendous infusion of American capital into Mexico; this wave of investments was especially pronounced in some of the northern Mexican states immediately below the border, as indicated by the following tables.

Thus, the official border that separated the United States from Mexico was, to some extent, a fictional device. As in the case of the effective penetration of the old borderlands, the expansion of capitalism proceeded below the border set by the Treaty of Guadalupe-Hidalgo.

Of course, there were a few differences in the new process. First, the process of capitalist expansion below the border was erratic rather than continuous. The Civil War in the United States and the open resistance of Mexican authorities forced a slower pace. As the same time, expansionism had to consider the uprooted peoples who disrupted the frontier for many years. These early years of development in the border area took place under constant threat of forceful conquest by the United States. In the end, American business monopolies accomplished this goal without open resort to armed strength.

As the century came to a close, little economic development had taken place along the border in spite of United States' capitalist penetration. The railroads had only recently interrupted the isolation characteristic of the area, and the basic system of land tenure remained unaffected. During this period, the northern states of Mexico began to suffer from the alliance of two different economic systems: American capitalism, rapidly advancing into its monopoly phase, and the backward latifundismo which had become even more entrenched under the leadership of Porfirio Díaz. In this setting, the growth and development of the border towns and the border area began.

TABLE 1

Basic Calendar of American Economic Penetration
into Areas Adjacent to the Border

Early 1880s	William Cornell Green purchases the Cananea Mines and organizes the Green Consolidated Copper Company.
April, 1887–Sept., 1888	2,077 new mining claims and 33 stamp mills appear over all of Mexico.
1888	$30,000,000 is invested in mining. Solomon R. Guggenheim purchases several silver mines.
1890	Solomon and William Guggenheim build the first complete silver-lead smelting works in Monterrey, Mexico.

TABLE 2

Total U.S. Investments in Mexico by State in 1902

D.F.	$320,852,000 ($281,000,000 in railroads)
(border) Coahuila	48,000,000
(border) Sonora	37,500,000
(border) Chihuahua	32,000,000
Oaxaca	14,000,000
(border) Nuevo León	11,000,000
Sinalva	7,000,000
Durango	7,000,000
Veracruz	4,455,000
Guanajuato	3,000,000
(border) Baja Calif.	2,374,000

TABLE 3

U.S. Investments by Branch in 1902

Railways	70%
Mining	$95,000,000
Agriculture	28,000,000
Manufacturing	10,000,000
Banks	7,000,000
Smelting Refineries	7,000,000
Utilities	6,000,000
Total (1,177 companies, firms and individuals)	$500,000,000

TABLE 4

Mining Investments by State in 1902

Sonora	$27,829,000
Chihuahua	21,277,000
D.F.	8,430,000
Durango	6,520,000
Coahuila	6,000,000
Aguascalientes	3,682,000
Sinaloa	3,183,000

TABLE 5

Agricultural Interests by State in 1902

Oaxaca	$10,700,000
Sonora	3,733,000
Veracruz	3,513,000
Chihuahua	1,822,000
Tabasco	1,506,000
Chiapas	1,188,000

TABLE 6

Representative Firms in the Border Area

Mining

W.A. Clark Menator from Montana	Copper Mines	$ 220,000
	Sonora	222,000
		442,000
Creston-Colorado Gold Mining Company	Sonora	2,222,000
Greene Consolidated Copper Company	Sonora	7,500,000
Moctzume & Phelps Dodge	Sonora	2,000,000
Las Cruces of New York & Sonora Mining Co.	Sonora	444,000
Sinaloa and Sonora Mining & Smelting	Sonora	600,000

Smelting

American Smelting & Refining Company (Guggenheim)	Monterrey Nuevo León	6,000,000
" "	Coahuila	750,000
" "	Chihuahua	600,000

Haciendas, ranchos, and farms

Mrs. Phoebe A. Hearst	Chihuahua	1,333,000
Nelson Welle Company	Coahuila	436,000
Greene Cattle Company	Sonora	—
A.M. Sherman	—	500,000 acres

Source: Tables 1 through 6 were culled from James M. Callahan, *American Foreign Policy in Mexican Relations* (New York: Cooper Square, 1968).

v: Border Economy 1: The Framework of Migration

The purpose of the chapter is not to study Mexican migration in particular, or specific aspects of Mexican migration in detail but rather to place Mexican migration across the border in perspective in a threefold sense. First of all, by showing the intimate connection that existed and still exists between the pattern of agricultural landholding in California (the material dealt with in the first chapter) and the development of Mexican migration. Secondly, by showing how this landholding pattern and the need for cheap labor affect the whole of the phenomenon of migration to California much before the onset of massive Mexican migration. And thirdly, by showing how the occurrence of massive migrations was not unique to the border between the United States and Mexico, but became part and parcel of the web of relationships between rich and poor countries during and after the development of large capitalist monopolies in land and agriculture. There is already a vast and growing body of literature on such important specific topics as the Bracero Program, commuters, etc. In general, this literature deals primarily with Mexican migration and usually a very specific aspect of Mexican migration. By contrast, the intention of this chapter is to provide neither a summary of this literature nor a research contribution to it; it is rather an effort to set down a number of elements that must be included as constituent parts of a theoretical explanation of Mexican migration to the United States and to show the manner in which, historically, migration is organically connected with the earlier economic development in the former Mexican and Spanish northwest. Thus, the cursory treatment given to specific aspects of Mexican migration per se is not an indication of lack of regard for the importance of these topics, but a consequence of the conscious decision to examine *general* and not *particular* aspects as the title indicates.

To accomplish these goals, it is necessary to clarify the social property relations that characterize an advanced capitalist economy. The notion of private property is usually regarded as the sine qua non of capitalism. However, the much too general sense attached to the popular notion of private property disguises a deeper reality that characterizes any predominantly capitalist society. Property in the *means of production*, e.g., land, equipment, tools, etc., is the privilege of one group or class in the society. The other class is dispossessed and owns no property in this particular sense. Thus the only effective ownership that a person of the latter class can exercise is ownership over his/her own ability to labor, i.e., labor power.

Whenever and wherever this class separation does not exist, capitalism cannot develop. This is the reason why an economic "theorist" of the nineteenth century, Edward Gibbon Wakefield, was very critical of the early development of the United States. In his view, the ability of the potential wage-worker, who arrived as a migrant on the East Coast, to migrate into the interior of the United States and become a self-employed farmer was the gravest obstacle in the development of capitalism:

> Where land is very cheap and all men are free, where everyone who so pleases can easily obtain a piece of land for himself, not only is labour very dear . . . but the difficulty *is* to obtain labour at any price.[1]

One way to remedy this situation was to prevent all men from being free, as happened in the slave South. As the nineteenth century wore on, however, the waves of migrants arriving upon the eastern seashore vastly outnumbered the ability of migrants to settle in the interior. Therefore, the lack of a pool of "free labor" ceased to be a deterrent to the advance of capitalism, while in the South slavery was abolished.[2]

What were the parameters of a) ownership in land and b) availability of labor in the Southwest after the Anglo-American conquest and the establishment of the new border? As we have established in previous chapters the characteristic landed monopolies that prevailed in the Southwest during the Spanish and Mexican periods changed hands but remained largely intact in the transition from Mexico to the United States. From a feudal monopoly in the land the economy of the southwestern states was swiftly transformed into one characterized by capitalist monopoly of the land. To the heritage of the Spanish and Mexican period we must add a development in the American economy which was to reinforce the absence of the small farmstead in the far Southwest: the development of imperialist monopoly capitalism.

This development can be described in its general and particular manifestations. In its general aspects it consisted of the loss of importance, at the national level, of the small competitive firm, its replacement by the large industrial monopolies, the growing importance of financial institutions, the fusion of financial and industrial concerns and the growth of capital exports. In its particular aspect in the Southwest it meant the concentration of land ownership and the intervention of bank capital in the promotion and direction of agricultural production.

The concentration that already existed in the Spanish land-grants was augmented through a series of economic policies and events such as the railroad grants and land speculation which transformed the Southwest, especially California, into an empire of large farms. Thus, from the outset, whoever was not the owner of a portion of this empire was a landless peasant and potential wage-worker. In part, it was this pattern of land distribution coupled with a very low population density that made California and the Southwest, after aridity had been conquered by irrigation, dependent upon foreign migrant labor.

Carey McWilliams, writing in the late 1930s, could look back to the history of California agriculture and describe it as the history of Asian-American migration. Today Mexican migration seems to have always been the rule, but the fact that less than forty years ago a social critic could look back eighty years and refer not to Mexican but to Asian labor as the prototype suggests that there was nothing special about Mexican labor per se and that the fundamental needs for large masses of cheap labor were inherent in the growing agribusiness empire.[3] Asian labor was utilized in California agriculture after some of the crops that were earlier cultivated such as coffee, tobacco, and silk, were abandoned. Other early crops were not terribly dependent on large pools of labor. While some labor scarcity was already apparent in the 1850s, it was therefore, not yet critical. With the growing of specialized fruit crops in the 1860s and 1870s, immigrant Chinese workers became indispensable in California agriculture. But a combination of organized labor and small farming interests, appealing to racism, succeeded in driving the Chinese from the California fields. The large California growers, in search of a new source of labor, promptly found one in the Japanese, who became a prime labor pool from the last few years of the nineteenth century to the beginning of World War I. But the Japanese were to meet the same opposition as the Chinese and eventually shared the same fate. In desperation, California agribusiness began to import East Indian and Filipino workers. Asian labor continued to provide the bulk of the labor needs of California agriculture until "the discovery of the Mexican" in the mid-1920s.

As well as the social property relations that prevailed in the Southwest, importance should be accorded to the scientific and technical discoveries that made the production of certain crops economically possible. Among these were the development of refrigerator cars that permitted the transportation of fresh produce to distant markets and the development of large-scale irrigation. The change from wheat production to specialized deciduous fruits and truck gardening in California was dependent on these developments. But nothing equals in impact the influence that the growth of large-scale irrigation had on the Southwest as a whole. Large-scale irrigation signified in itself a tremendous development of the productive forces. In 1902, the Southwest, an area larger in size than the original American thirteen colonies, was little more than an unpopulated desert. In 1902, the Reclamation Act, which made possible the use of federal funds for the construction of large irrigation projects, was passed, marking the beginning of the modern economic development of the Southwest. Irrigation allowed the reclamation of millions of previously arid and unproductive acres and helped turn large portions of desert brush country into fertile orchards.

Such an expansion of acreage and the ability to grow cotton and truck produce in previously uncultivated areas in itself necessitated increased labor supplies. Large-scale irrigation meant, additionally, a new and increased over-capitalization of the land. Heavy capital investment, in addition to creating "agribusiness" by bringing banking capital into the agricultural enterprise, meant an increased demand for ever larger pools of cheap labor.

If these were the parameters in terms of productive forces and productive relations north of the border, what were the conditions south of the border at the time of the onset of large Mexican migration? A number of circumstances coincided in the Mexican economy around the turn of the century to condition the northward migration. One was the process of depeasanting agrarian Mexico that became especially rigorous during the Díaz regime. Throughout the second half of the nineteenth century Mexico suffered the pangs of its peculiar form of primitive capitalist accumulation.[4] The expropriation of the property of the Church and Indian communities are phenomena which must be understood as part of this process. The disentailment law, which presumed to create small agricultural holdings, in fact brought about the further concentration of land and the opening of a market in land transaction. The activities of the famous "compañías deslindadoras" also formed part of the process of primitive accumulation. The

Yaqui wars which deprived those Indians of their fertile lands in the Yaqui valley gave a "colonial" character to this process by producing the landless peasant.[5]

The railroads were the second element in the genesis of Mexican migration: they enabled the landless peasant to find a wage-earning job. They were instrumental in bringing the peasants to labor markets, such as the American operated mines of northern Mexico and eventually to the larger labor markets of the United States. If the process of depeasanting gave them their "freedom" to move and the railroads provided the means of transportation, the Mexican Revolution of 1911 sent them in droves across the border.

From the above description of the conditions at the onset of Mexican migration to the United States one might draw the conclusion that this movement of people was and is a unique phenomenon of modern economic history. Nothing could be further from the truth. One of the marks of the development of monopoly capitalism in the United States and Europe was the development of migration from backward to advanced capitalist countries as well as the appearance of a new wave of "white settler" colonialism. Germany at the turn of the century is an example of the generality of this phenomenon. This has been pointed out by Handman:

> Germany . . . presents an analogy with the agricultural labor situation of the Mexican in America. . . . Germany, particularly in the East, had large landed estates which needed additional seasonal labor in order to produce for a growing market. In proportion, however, as the cities and industrial life made calls on the working forces of the country, the large landowners and producers began to call in seasonal labor from (other) regions. . . . the result was that Germany before the War imported annually more than four hundred thousand agricultural laborers to harvest her crops.[6]

For American agribusiness north of the border the Mexican migrant was better than any previous migrant. The ideal immigrant was one who showed up for harvest work and who "disappeared" in the off-season. This ideal immigrant would not cost society the expense of bringing him up and would not become a public "nuisance." The early Asian migrants met the ideal requirements for only a brief period of time. Given the physical distance to their homelands it was natural that they should settle permanently in the United States. Worse yet, they promptly began to leave the workfields to settle either on small farms purchased with savings, or in cities where they became self-employed businessmen.

Given the formidable need for cheap labor that was felt during the early part of the century, the Mexican migrants appeared to hold superior qualities: availability in larger numbers and disappearance in the off-season made possible through easy return to Mexico. Although it turned out that some Mexican migrants, like their Asian predecessors, chose on occasion to settle in the United States, from the point of view of agribusiness Mexican migration was "better" than its predecessors. Also, important differentiations should be made within Mexican migration. The most important separation is between legal and illegal migrants. It is the latter type that most perfectly fits the "job description" of the agricultural (or industrial) hand. The illegal entrant is available in large numbers whenever and wherever he is needed and is completely at the mercy of immigration authorities when he is not wanted. The illegal migrant does not require education, training, or sustenance (except for the portion of the year during which he works), the costs of his rearing are borne by his home country; and because of his legal status—the fact that he can be deported at a moment's notice—he is likely to be a "loyal," if not an especially hard-working, laborer.

Not all the migration from Mexico has been illegal, however. The most famous example of legal migration is the bracero program, whereby the needs of agriculture in the Southwest were met through a legalized system of contract labor. Looking back at the history of sixty-plus years of Mexican migration, it appears that migration was very intense between 1910–30; it declined relatively between 1930–50, only to rise again in the last twenty years. It is during this last period that illegal migration became a factor of paramount importance in the economics and politics of the area. Strictly speaking the "illegal" phase in Mexican migration started during and after the Second World War.

Throughout these sixty years all the socio-economic conditions that were present at the outset have been of continuing influence. With the exception of an actual revolutionary war in Mexico, all the other factors remain in force in modified form: the capitalization of southwestern agriculture continues unabated: means of transportation to and from Mexico have improved considerably and, despite legal changes in land tenure in Mexico, the poverty of the small peasant still acts as a factor in his migration. One major new element has appeared in the whole framework: the development of urbanization along the United States-Mexico border.

This process of urbanization matches the urbanization of those Mexican migrants who have settled in the United States. From the perspective of the development of large towns in the Mexican border area two particular forms of migratory movements are of interest. One is the case of illegal migrants whose movement is facilitated enormously by the existence of large urban centers, which serve as bases of operations. The second type is the so-called commuter: a person who lives in Mexico but who crosses the border every day to work in the United States. Both of these types of migrants have contributed to the settlement of northern Mexico; and, conversely, they have made their appearance in the United States in large numbers *on the basis of* such a process of urbanization. As such, the "illegals" and the "commuters" are both *cause and consequence* of the rise of the border towns. It is in this sense that the urbanization of northern Mexico and the migration northward are inseparable. Whereas migration of all types provided for much of the urban settlement of the border area, now the border area in turn has become the source of a new and important form of migration.

vi: *Border Economy 2: Urbanization and Border Towns*

The urbanization brought about by the migratory process we have described was not peculiar to the northern border area of Mexico. Rather it was a particular manifestation of the general development of migration and urbanization in Mexico since the 1920s, and especially since World War II. Despite all of its important singular characteristics, the border economy of northern Mexico shares some fundamental aspects of the Mexican economy as a whole. An analysis of the problems confronting Mexico's north must therefore be preceded by a presentation of the outstanding socio-economic features of contemporary Mexico.

The Mexican Economy at the Crossroads

At present the Mexican economy is affected by some important "developmental" traits. Chief among these are: the monopolistic structure of the economy; the presence of perhaps the strongest "state-capitalist sector" in all of Latin America; an agrarian structure which preserves wide disparities of income and wealth among the rural population; cities filled with vast masses of the unemployed and underemployed; and last, but not least, a strong economic relationship with the United States, in which the latter country exercises dominance. These traits characterized Mexico ten years ago and, despite a decade of rapid growth, the evils connected with these structural elements have not been alleviated. In fact, conditions have worsened.

Monopoly—concentration in industrial production, agriculture and finance—constitutes the primary characteristic of Mexico's semicapitalist economy.[1] Of 135,000 industrial enterprises examined by the VIII Censo Industrial of 1965 a minute 0.82 percent accounted for 64.3 of the total production and 66.3 percent of the total capital investment for that year. The same monopolistic structure is present in the agricultural sector of the Mexican economy: in 1960, 3 percent of the farms (or 79,000 out of a total of 2.5 million) produced 55 percent of all agricultural produce and accounted for 80 percent of the increase in value of production since the 1950s (Table 7). Equally concentrated is the financial sector of the economy where six large commercial banks control 83.4 percent of all deposits. Hand-in-hand with monopoly, the state (the "public sector") has come to play an important role in all sectors of the Mexican economy. As of November 1973 there were over four hundred fifty state enterprises operating in Mexico some of which were the largest in the economy. Early in the 1960s the role played by the Mexican state was already impressive: at that time the state owned all of the nation's ten largest enterprises, 88.5 percent of the twenty largest and 82.5 percent of the thirty largest (Table 8).

The agrarian structure set up by the Mexican agrarian reform law allowed a surreptitious concentration of land which has permitted a relatively small number of landowners and farmers to benefit from credit facilities, price support programs, etc., while the vasy majority of the beneficiaries received a subfamily plot. But the predominantly monopolistic structure of the economy has not facilitated the absorption of an increasing surplus working force, and thus unemployment and income disparities have continued to afflict Mexico. In Mexico today the average income of the richest 5 percent of families is thirty-six times as great as that of the poorest 10 percent of families, whereas it was thirty times as great twenty years ago. The wealthiest tenth of the population receives over

TABLE 7

Proportional Distribution of Production and Resources, 1960

Type of Holding	Number of Plots	Value of Production	Value of Plots[a]	Cultivable Area	Value of Machinery	Irrigated Area	% of Farmers Receiving Credits[b]	Contribution to Increased Production between 1950–1960
Total	100.0	100.0	100.0	100.0	100.0	100.0	51.5	100.0
Infra-subsistence	50.3	4.2	6.7	13.6	1.3	—	20.5	−1
Subfamily	33.8	17.1	13.8	24.5	6.5	3.9	28.2	10
Family	12.6	24.4	22.6	19.2	17.0	27.0	58.1	11
Multifamily Medium	2.8	22.0	19.3	14.4	31.5	31.5	62.6	35
Multifamily Large	0.5	32.3	37.6	28.3	43.7	37.6	75.0	45

[a]The value of the plot is composed of the value of the land, or fixed and semifixed capital, and of livestock. By plot is meant the ejidal plots (not the whole ejido) and the nonejidal plots.

[b]Based on a regional sample survey and judged not to be representative of the nation as a whole.

Source: Centro de Investigaciones Agrarias, *Estructura agraria y desarrollo agrícola en Mexico*, vol. 1, p. 296, vol. 3, pp. 14–20.

TABLE 8

(A)

Mexico's Largest Industrial Firms, 1965
(measured by total production)

| Firms | Control of Total Production (%) | |
	(of the 938)	(of the country)
Top 10	17.7	11.0
Top 100	49.4	30.6
Top 300	72.2	44.7
All	100.0	62.0

(B)

Distribution of 938 Largest Industrial Firms
by Composition of Capital, 1965

| Firms | Degree of Control of Total Production (%) | | | |
	Foreign	State	Private National	Total
Top 10	50.0	20.0	30.0	100.0
Top 20	55.0	15.0	30.0	100.0
Top 50	48.0	22.0	30.0	100.0
Top 100	47.0	13.0	40.0	100.0
Top 500	31.0	7.4	61.6	100.0
All	26.7	5.1	68.0	100.0

Source: Taken from David Barkin, "Mexico's Albatross: the U.S. Economy,"
in *Latin American Perspectives* 2, no. 2, p. 67.

one-half of the income while the poorest one-half of the population enjoys 15 percent of Mexico's total personal income (Table 9). Thus the urban areas of Mexico—the "underdeveloped cities"—are the concentrated focuses of all the evils usually associated with "backwardness" or "underde-

TABLE 9

Distribution of Family Incomes in Mexico, 1950, 1958, 1963, 1969
(in percentages)

Deciles* (10% of Families)	1950		1958		1963		1969		Average Monthly Income (1969 price)		
	By Decile	Cumulative	By Decile	Cumulative	By Decile	Cumulative	By Decile	Cumulative	1950	1958	1963
I	2.7	2.7	2.2	2.0	2.0	2.0	2.0	374	437	457	518
II	2.4	6.1	2.8	5.0	2.2	4.2	2.0	4.0	472	545	
III	3.8	9.9	3.3	8.3	3.2	7.4	3.0	7.0	527	638	745
IV	4.4	14.3	3.9	12.2	3.7	11.1	3.5	10.5	610	745	865
V	4.8	19.1	4.5	16.7	4.6	15.7	4.5	15.0	665	880	1,069
VI	5.5	24.6	5.5	22.2	5.2	20.9	5.0	20.0	760	1,140	1,208
VII	7.0	31.6	6.3	28.5	6.6	27.5	7.0	27.0	968	1,220	1,528
VIII	8.6	40.2	8.6	37.1	9.9	37.4	9.0	36.0	1,190	1,660	2,308
IX	10.8	51.0	13.6	50.7	12.7	50.1	13.0	49.0	1,498	2,632	2,960
X**	49.0	100.0	49.3	100.0	49.9	100.0	51.0	100.0	6,790	9,560	11,615
90–95%	8.8		10.7		11.6		15.0		2,450	4,124	5,395
95–100%	40.2		38.6		38.3		36.0		11,110	14,975	17,850
Total	100.0		100.0		100.0		100.0		1,385	1,935	2,328
Gini Coefficient	0.50		0.53		0.55		0.58				

*Each decile represents 510,500 families for 1950; 640,510 for 1958; 732,960 for 1963; and 889,114 for 1969.

**The last decile at the top of the scale of income has been divided into two parts of 5% each.

Sources: Ifigenia M. de Navarrete, "La distribución del ingreso en Mexico," in *El Perfil de México en 1980–I* (Mexico, Siglo XXI editores, 1970). 1969–1970 family income survey with adjustments.

velopment": unemployment, underemployment, rapid urban growth, deterioration of social services, etc.

The degree of United States business influence on the workings of the economy can be gleaned from two separate but combined aspects of foreign investment in Mexico: foreign industrial capital and foreign loan capital. As a first approximation, Table 10 gives an indication of the importance of *direct* foreign capital among the largest Mexican enterprises. The abundance of large foreign enterprises is due to the rapid inroads made by the transnational corporations in Mexico in the last fifteen years. According to a Harvard University survey of the U.S. multinational corporations that account for the bulk of U.S. foreign direct investment in manufacturing, 162 of these companies were installed in Mexico in 1967 with 4.2

TABLE 10

Fifty Largest Companies in Mexico
(based on capitalization)
1970

Company	Principal Shareholder	Capital (million pesos)
1. Teléfonos de Mexico	Government	3,070
2. Banco Nac. Agropecuario	Government	1,500
3. Cía. Mex. de Luz y Fuerza	Government	1,361
4. Nacional Financiera	Government	1,300
5. CONASUPO	Government	1,000
6. Guanos y Fertilizantes	Government	1,000
7. Banco Nal. de Crédito Agr.	Government	850
8. Altos Hornos de Mex.	Government	800
9. Imp. de Papaloapán	Government	750
10. Cía Fundidora de Mty	Banco Nacional de Mexico (BNM)	675
11. Celanese Mexicana	BNM-Celanese	642
12. Financiera Banamex	BNM	640
13. Hojalata y Lamina	Garza Sada	580
14. ANDSA	Government	500
15. Banco de México	Government	500

Table 10 Continued:

16. Banco Nal. de Obras y Serv. Pub.	Government	500
17. Cervecería Modelo	BNM (P. Diez)	500
18. Soc. Mex. Cre. Industrial	Government	500
19. Banco Nacional de México	BNM	475
20. Cervecería Cuauhtemoc	Garza-Laguera	440
21. Fertilizantes Fosfatados	BNM-Government-Panamerican Sulphur	440
22. Tubos de Acero de México	Government	406
23. Asarco Mexicana	American Smelting	400
24. Banco de Comercio	Banco de Comercio	400
25. Celulosa de Chihuahua	Banco Comercial Mexicano	400
26. Cementos Tolteca	British Cement Mfgrs.	400
27. HYLSA de Mexico		385
28. Sears Roebuck	Sears	375
29. Financiera Bancomer	Banco de Comercio	360
30. Banco Nal. de Cre. Ejidal	Government	350
31. Cía Cigarrera la Moderna	Brown & Williamson	350
32. Cervecería Moctezuma	Banco Commercial Mexicano	330
33. Cía Industrial de Atenquique	Government	300
34. Cía Mexicana del Cobre	Government	300
35. Puerto de Liverpool		300
36. Fábricas Automex	Chrysler	300
37. Ford Motor Company	Ford	300
38. Kodak Industrial	Kodak	300
39. Volkswagen de Mexico	Volkswagen	300
40. Anderson Clayton	Anderson Clayton	290
41. Fierro Esponja	Hojalata y Lamina-Garza Sada	290
42. Unives	—	254
43. Cementes Anahuac	BNM—J Serrano	250
44. Diesel Nacional	Government	250
45. Lever de Mexico	Unilever (UK)	250
46. Cía Nestlé	Nestle	240
47. Cía Minera de Cananea	—	240
48. Valores Industriales		240
49. Industrias Unidas	Ing. Alejo Poralta	235
50. Cigarros El Aguila	British-American Tobacco	230

Source: Barkin, "Mexico's Albatross."

subsidiaries. Of the total number of subsidiaries, 225 were in the manufacturing sector; 143 were completely new firms while 221 were either acquisitions or branches of other previously established business.[2] The influx of multinational corporations brought about an accelerated pace of foreign investment and, during the 1960s the book value of private foreign investment increased from $1,080 million to $2,300 million in 1968—an increase of over 100 percent in the space of ten years. The trend of the investment pattern during these years was away from traditional sectors such as public services and mining and toward trade, tourism, and manufacturing. The quick pace of foreign penetration, especially as U.S. corporations made their way through direct purchase into the most dynamic sectors of local industry, was another characteristic of the 1960s. This trend occurred most notably in consumer durables, chemicals, electronics, department stores, hotels and restaurants, and the food industry, in which United Fruit, Heinz, and General Foods became very visible.

The process of denationalization and control can best be illustrated by the role of Anderson Clayton in the Mexican economy. Anderson Clayton's role in the Mexican agriculture places it among the top twenty corporations (government companies not included) when measured by reported capital. This company controls, through credit and marketing channels, the production of cotton, which is Mexico's leading export product. Anderson Clayton provides more credit for cotton production than the National Edijal bank gives to all of Mexico ejidatarios. The control over the production of cotton is made effective because the Mexican producers do not sell their cotton production in the international markets but do it mostly through Anderson Clayton (also through Hohenberg International, MacFadden, and other U.S. based enterprises) which monopolize the harvest and provide credit, seed, and fertilizers to the producers. The company also controls cotton production in the countries with which Mexico must compete: Brazil and the U.S. Anderson Clayton thus has engaged in cotton "dumping" to remind Mexico who is in control.[3] In recent years Anderson Clayton has branched out into Mexican production of cattle feed, chocolates, planting seeds, edible oils, and insecticides. Other U.S. corporations have joined Anderson Clayton in effectively taking over Mexico's agribusiness, from production and sale of machinery and fertilizers to the processing and merchandising of agricultural goods. Among the better known are John Deere, International Harvester, Celanese, Monsanto, Dupont, American Cyanamid, Corn Products, United Fruit, and Ralston Purina.[4]

A less visible form of foreign control is effected through foreign loan capital. The total foreign debt of Mexico has expanded considerably in recent years, reaching the figure of $11 billion in late 1972; $5 billion of this amount were credits by U.S. private banks; $1.47 billion came from the Export-Import Bank, the World Bank, and the Inter-American development bank; and $1.5 billion from European, Canadian, and Japanese banks. More than half (55 percent) of the foreign debt was absorbed by private American commercial banks. Between 1950 and 1972 the foreign debt grew at an average rate of 23 percent.[5]

There are several reasons for the large size and rate of growth of the foreign debt of Mexico. First of all, the application to Mexico, and to the rest of Latin America, of the economic policies propounded around 1950 by the Economic Commission for Latin America must be taken into consideration. The essence of the ECLA analysis is well-known. Mexico, Latin America, in general, and other primary-commodity producers had ceased to benefit from free trade and the international division of labor. This was due to factors such as "income inelasticities" for primary goods which, coupled with the effects of union demands in the industrialized countries, resulted in both a deterioration of the terms of trade and chronic balance-of-payments difficulties for most Latin American nations. The policy recommendation for the resolution of this thorny problem became known as "import-substitution industrialization" (ISI).[6] A policy to favor import substitution through protective tariffs on industrial imports was taken to be the direct route to industrialization. After flourishing from the late 1940s to the early 1960s, the policies of ISI were pronounced dead. ISI failed in its goals, and economic conditions had become, if anything, worse than before. Unemployment continued unabated; ISI industries had not penetrated the export markets; and the dependence upon the export of primary products became intensified, for now the import mix showed a higher degree of semifinished materials, spare parts, and machinery necessary for the maintenance of ISI industries.

The policies of ECLA during this period resulted in a true substitution of imports, although not in the sense ostensibly defended by ECLA theorists. The whole ISI period provided a resolution for a problem of markets confronting the predominantly monopolistic economics of the U.S. and other advanced countries. The chronic balance of payments difficulties of Latin American nations made their purchase of finished consumer goods in the United States a precarious and unpredictable activity. ISI provided market stability by bringing foreign capital (usually with foreign machinery and raw materials) into production in Latin America, where products that had been imported for half of a century were now produced and sold. In the meantime, new credits were issued for the importation of machinery and raw materials (this was the actual import substitution!) based upon the high expectations for growth in the ISI industries. It was not long before the new industries had passed their high growth-rate and new bottlenecks to development appeared in the form of "limited internal markets," which prevented the further growth of domestic industry.[7]

But in the end the policy of ISI did not improve balance-of-payment difficulties of Mexico. In place of consumer goods purchased directly from foreign producers, raw materials, intermediate goods, and capital equipment imports skyrocketed to provision the numerous factories catering to the sumptuary demands of the oligarchy and the affluent middle classes, comprising as much as 30 percent of the entire population. The chronic balance-of-payment problem became aggravated, moreover, by mounting repatriation of profits and other income by foreign investors, by the increase in the ratio

TABLE 11

Rates of Profit and Profit Repatriation in Manufacturing

| | % Profit | | % Profit Repatriation | |
	1969	1970	1969	1970
Latin America	12.0%	11.0%	6.0%	6.1%
Mexico	10.3	9.6	5.4	6.7
Argentina	12.4	7.8	9.0	7.6
Brazil	12.3	14.0	5.2	5.7
Chile	Loss	1.5	—	—
Colombia	10.8	8.6	4.6	5.9
Peru	7.2	8.3	4.2	4.1
Venezuela	16.2	14.2	6.0	8.4

Source: *Hanson's Latin American Letter*, Washington, no. 1392, Nov. 20, 1971.

and total volume of reinvestment of earnings rather than new foreign investment by foreign firms and, finally, by the practice of "over-pricing" and "over-invoicing" of transnational corporations. A brief digression on the last item is necessary to illustrate the power of the multinational corporations.

The obvious discrepancy between the official low rates of profit (see Table 11) made public for foreign companies and the eagerness with which foreign capital has gone into certain sectors caused the government of Colombia to commission an investigation of the subject. In the Colombian study it was discovered, for example, that a given amount of chemical product that sold for $100 in the world market, was "sold" by the parent member of a multinational complex to its Colombian subsidiary at an average of $255. The ability to perform this kind of operation is one of the great advantages that imperialism has obtained through the medium of the so-called multinationals. A growing portion of world trade is carried on presently by the branches of the multinational corporations; and the prices utilized in such transactions are bogus, serving the ultimate purpose of covering up and shifting profits from country to country.[8] The order of magnitude of the differential in profit rates accounted for by intracorporate transfer pricing is shown in Table 12. It should be noted that the multinational corporation is very *flexible* in its transfer pricing policies. In the case of sales of oil from subsidiaries to the parent company, the transfer of profits via overpricing usually favors the less developed country—a reverse practice which allows the parent companies to solicit larger benefits from the United States Internal Revenue Service.

In an effort to remedy balance-of-payment problems it is natural that governments in the capitalist world should welcome off-setting foreign investments. But the "nationalistic" policies of the PRI in Mexico, geared to presenting an image of an independent national capitalist class, have made the state the principal shareholder in a variety of institutions, and this situation has forced the state to utilize foreign debt as one of the means of its "Mexicanization" policy.

Mexico as a whole is thus characterized by a monopolistic structure that is both rural and urban; by the predominance of a state capitalist sector which appears to be in the clutches of the American commercial banks on which it must rely as sources of funding; and by an industrial-urban structure that is unable to raise (a) the level of employment or (b) the amount

TABLE 12

Profit Rates of Foreign Companies in Colombia, 1968

Type of Industry	Average Rate of Overpricing	Official Profit Rate	Effective Profit Rate
Pharmaceutical	155%	6.7	79.1
Rubber	40	16.0	43.0
Chemical	25.5	n.d.	n.d.
Electronic	16-66	n.d.	n.d.

Source: C.V. Vaitsos, "Transfer of Resources and Preservation of Monopoly Rents," Center for International Affairs, Harvard University, *Economic Development Report 168,* 1970.

of manufactured exports that well deserves the title of the "ciudad subdesarrollada."

The Mexican economy is thoroughly influenced industrially and financially by American-based multinational corporations and American banks. In its efforts to appear to free itself from the penetration of direct U.S. and foreign capital, Mexico had to give in to the control of international bank capital. To free itself of the balance-of-payments problem and the burden of the foreign debt, the Mexican government must strive to increase both its agricultural and manufactured exports. It must also try to increase revenue from foreign tourists, and strive to reduce the consumption of foreign goods by its citizens, while maintaining the pattern of consumption, production, and distribution of social wealth which predominates at present. The problems and contradictions of the economy as a whole find direct expression in the northern border area, and, as we shall see, the proposed remedies for the national ills are "at work" in this area.

The Basic Economic Life of the "Border Town" and Its Environs

The Mexican border states and the border zone itself have experienced a tremendous growth in population and urbanization over the last fifty years. This growth has affected the make-up of some very old towns such as Nuevo Laredo, and it has been the major force in the development of wholly new urban centers such as Tijuana. The eight major municipalities of the Mexican border are from west to east, Tijuana, Mexicali, Nogales, Ciudad Juárez, Piedras Negras, Nuevo Laredo, Reynosa, and Matamoros. Between 1950 and 1960 the total population of these eight centers increased by 83 percent, from less than nine hundred thousand to 1.5 million (data includes Ensenada). By 1970 the population had reached a total of 2.3 million persons or about 5 percent of the total population of Mexico. Between 1960 and 1969 the population rise in the northern border states (Baja California, Sonora Chihuahua, Coahuila, Nuevo León, and Tamaulipas) grew by

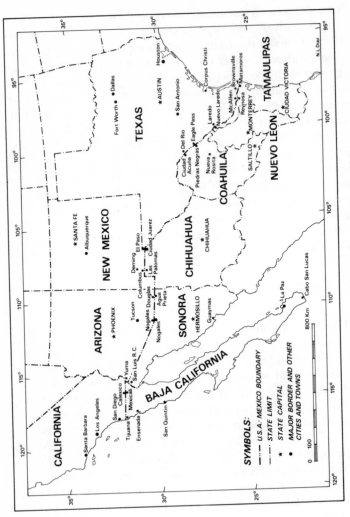

The United States–Mexico Border (1977)

45 percent in contrast with a figure of 31 percent for the nation as a whole. During the 1950s the rates of growth of the largest cities on the border surpassed that of the Federal District, and the growth continues unabated today. As shown in the previous chapter, this increase in population and rate of population growth has been due fundamentally to migration. In 1970, fully 29 percent of the border population came from other parts of the country, and foreigners accounted for another 2 percent.

The population of the northern states is concentrated predominantly in the cities listed above and several other urban centers. In this regard the northern states are more highly urbanized than Mexico as a whole. The outstanding example is the state of Baja California where 85 percent of the state's population is urban, living in localities of twenty-five hundred or more inhabitants.

The physical conditions of the area are such that the population is largely concentrated in four cities (Tijuana, Mexicali, Ensenada, Tecate) in the northern part of the state, the rest of the area being practically uninhabited. Only half a century ago the entire area of Baja California was practically uninhabited, but a number of historical events coincided to set off the growth that we still witness today. First of all, the continued fear of American attempts to annex Baja California caused the Mexican government to initiate various programs to encourage the settlement and colonization of the area during the 1910s and 1920s. As we have indicated, the penetration of the northern area of Mexico had proceeded apace during the regime of Porfirio Díaz and by 1885 "little that was Mexican remained" in Baja California.[9] As a reaction to the power of U.S. private interests in the area and various U.S. colonization projects, the government of Mexico realized that the only way to maintain sovereignty over the region was through a concerted colonization effort. Additionally, the licensing of gambling, the commercialization of vice, and opium refining became authorized activities that brought a large influx of population and gave to Tijuana the exotic character it still possesses.

As indicated in the previous chapter the origin of the growth has been such that these urban centers have never had the productive capacity needed to support such a large population. *The large concentrations of people in these towns perform the function of a large reserve of labor at the disposal of U.S. industry and agriculture.* The flow of labor services from Mexico into the United States has taken a variety of forms, but the specific flow from the border towns throughout the past decade and at the present time has been in the form of illegal migration and "commuters."

Illegal migration from Mexico is without a doubt the "best of all possible migrations." In the history of agribusiness in the Southwest the first preferred migrant agricultural workers were the Chinese and, later, the Japanese. Both groups seemed to make themselves scarce once the work duties ceased during the off-season. But this phenomenon turned out to be only an appearance, for the Chinese and the Japanese established themselves eventually as agriculturists and could not be depended upon to serve as a massive, highly mobile reserve of human labor. Their place was soon taken up by the Mexican migration. Since the motherland was much closer for Mexican migrant workers, it was anticipated that the Mexican migrant would be more apt to return to his homeland and not tend to settle in the United States. However, contrary to expectations, Mexicans not only settled in large numbers and became American citizens, but they also became highly urbanized. At this point, the *illegal* Mexican workers, apt to work in industry or in agriculture, raised at the expense of the Mexican economy, and easily deportable, came into the picture. Their presence has been felt especially since the end of World War II. At the present time the Immigration and Naturalization Service estimates that approximately 3 million illegal workers from Mexico come to work in the United States every year. These illegal workers have no recourse to the courts if they are exploited by employers and are willing to work for far lower wages than United States citizens can live on. Not all of these illegal workers make their permanent residence in the border towns, although the towns are used as a stopping point and base of operation.*

A source of labor more directly tied into the life of the border cities consists of the so-called green-card commuters. These are people who live in the border towns and who cross the border every day to work in the United States. The number of commuters varies a great deal from town to town. At the present time a conservative estimate places the number of green-card commuters at fifty thousand.[10] How important commuters' wages are as a source of labor revenue for workers residing in border towns is indicated in Table 13. In actuality, not only green-card commuters but many "illegal" workers cross the border every day to work in the United States, consequently accurate estimates of the total number of green-card holders plus illegals are unavailable at present.

TABLE 13

Mexican Border City Wages Earned in the United States

Mexican Border City	Percent of Total 1960 Wages Earned in U.S.
Matamoros	30
Reynosa	22
Nuevo Laredo	31
Piedras Negras	23
Ciudad Juárez	36
Nogales	19
Mexicali	21
Tijuana	33

Source: Secretaría de Comercio, *Programa Nacional Fronterizo,* Mexico, 1965.

*The reader is referred to the theoretical presentation of this material in the previous chapter.

The net result of the laboring activity of the large mass of workers concentrated south of the border is a depressing effect upon the wage rates and the maintenance of a higher-than-average level of unemployment in the areas of the United States bordering Mexico. Thus the fundamental aspect of the social economy of the border towns is the incorporation of a large pool of Mexican workers into the orbit of the American monopoly-capitalistic economy and the formation of a large reserve of competitive, unskilled and unorganized workers immediately south of the border. The most glaring economic appearance—a service oriented economy designed to satisfy the foreign visitor—is fully deceiving. The souvenir shops, peddlers, restaurants, night clubs, car watchers, barber and beauty shops, gasoline stations, store clerks, etc., are the visible facade that the border towns offer to the investigator. Beneath this facade one can discover something more elemental about the organization of material production in the United States.

The economic conditions that prevail in the *American* border area are a reflection of the fundamental aspect of the role of the laboring population in the economy. An indication of these conditions was the attention paid to border counties at the height of the War on Poverty in the late 1960s. The southern American border zone is characterized by the pressure of low-paid, foreign workers, small towns that depend on unsteady retail (and some wholesale) trade with Mexico, military establishments, agriculture based on irrigation, and higher than average unemployment rates. The basic categories of employment (military, agriculture, retail trade) are those where the organization of workers has traditionally been weakest. As opposed to the United States northern border with Canada—where industry, employment, union organization, and general economic conditions look like a cross-sectional reflection of the overall U.S. economy—the southern border appears to be a collection of aspects from the seamy side of the U.S. economy. This situation cannot be separated from the existence of Mexican underdevelopment.

Other Economic Activity across the Border Line

While the flow of labor resources northward is the principal element of the border equation, other elements are also important. Among these are the flow of Mexican workers' wages into retail establishments on the U.S. side of the border, the further dependence of this retail trade on purchases from a wider Mexican region, the flow of agricultural production from Mexican border states into the United States, the contribution of tourist dollars to the trade economy of Mexican border towns, the direct technological dependence of Mexican industry upon United States industry, and a host of illegal activities and enterprises.

A good portion of the income earned by residents of border towns is not spent in Mexico but in the United States. This is so regardless of the origin of the revenue. Thus the border towns provide not only a source of labor. The remuneration for this labor, and more, reverts back to American business, contributing to the uneven development of the area. A hypothetical Mexican family's binational shopping list is presented below (Table 14). The list indicates the relationship that exists between shopping patterns and differential availability of goods in retail stores on both sides of the border. The percentage of income that is spent on the U.S. side by Mexican nationals varies considerably. In one illustrative case it was estimated that the workers of American operated plants in Agua Prieta (Sonora) spent fully 52 percent of their gross income from wages in Douglas (Arizona) and other American towns.[11]

Expenditures by Mexican nationals in U.S.-side twin cities are not limited to local shoppers. The wholesale and retail establishments in these American border towns cater to a market that extends deep into Mexico. The town of Laredo on the Rio Grande, and also on a major highway that connects to the interior of Mexico, is one example of this far-reaching trade. It is said that wealthy Mexicans from Monterrey and beyond come to Laredo to make special purchases, mostly in the

TABLE 14

A Binational Shopping List

Buy in Mexico	Buy in U.S.
Services, including	Manufactured goods
Entertainment	Clothes
Physician's services	Cars
(particularly for	Car parts
Mexican-Americans)	Appliances
Dental Work	Canned goods
Some auto repairs	
Haircuts	
Staples	Poultry
Sugar	Eggs
Rice	
Most vegetables	American liquor
Tropical fruit	
Beef	American cigarettes
Baked goods	
Bottled beverages	
Liquor	
Beer	
Soft drinks	
Furniture	
Prescription drugs	

Source: David S. North, *The Border Crossers* (Washington, D.C.: Transcentury Corporation, 1970), p. 39.

clothing stores of this city. As a consequence, Laredo has the distinction of being the one U.S. city where apparel sales volume exceeds that of auto sales.[12] Nogales (Arizona), located on the Mexican West Coast Highway, attracts shoppers from several hundred miles south to its retail and wholesale outlets. Interviews conducted among businessmen in this city brought out the importance of purchases by Mexican nationals from as far away as Ciudad Obregón, Mazatlán, and Guadalajara. This pattern of trade obtains with variation in all border towns throughout the entire length of the border.

The border towns constitute the focal point of exchanges of agricultural goods flowing back and forth across the border. Recently, agricultural trade between the United States and Mexico has been on the increase. The Economic Research Service of the United States Department of Agriculture indicates that during 1973 agricultural trade between the United States and Mexico accelerated rapidly. U.S. agricultural exports to Mexico amounted to $254 million, 94 percent above 1972, and U.S. agricultural imports from Mexico totaled $706 million, up 32 percent. The U.S. is Mexico's principal supplier of farm imports. Mexico imports corn, grain, soybeans, fruits, vegetables, seeds, dairy products, poultry meats, and dairy cattle. At the same time, Mexico is the principal supplier of the U.S. domestic market for agricultural imports. The U.S. imports from Mexico cattle, beef, sugar, molasses, onions, tomatoes, melons, strawberries, fruits, and vegetables.

The obvious overlap between exports and imports is due in large part to the shipping of identical products back and forth across the border. Although this back-and-forth movement of commodities across the border reflects to some extent climactic conditions, e.g., the production of "winter vegetables" in Mexico, it is a relatively new phenomenon. As recently as the early 1940s the largest agricultural imports from Mexico by value were items not produced in the United States, such as bananas, coffee, chile, and henequen. The production of fresh vegetables for the U.S. market at this time was not as important as it is today. For instance, only a third of all the tomatoes produced were exported, although it should be pointed out that, even at

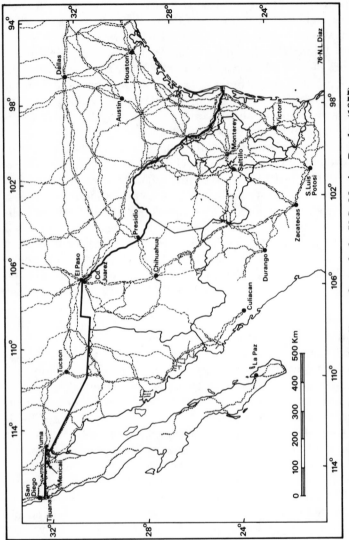

Major Highways and Railways through the U.S.–Mexico Border (1977)

this time, fully two-thirds of the production of two northern states (Sonora and Sinaloa) reached the American consumer. An important element in the appearance of the "winter vegetables"—and the two-way traffic of commodities through border towns—was the rapid development of "commercial agriculture" in the northern states of Mexico beginning in the early 1940s. With the building of the Pan-American Highway in Mexico the exports of tomatoes from the Mexican northeastern states increased from less than a million pounds in 1942 to 4 million pounds in 1943 and 14 million in 1944. Some of this early growth in production for export was based on the surplus production of small ejido parcels. By the late 1950s, however, full-fledged capitalist production of a variety of agricultural goods had developed—especially in Sonora, Sinaloa, and Tamaulipas. Thus a few small areas of northern Mexico have become pockets of California-like "agribusiness." Some of the crops that are produced in Mexico for export into the United States by Mexican workers, with the help of advanced agricultural methods and machinery are, during a different season of the year, produced in the United States for export to Mexico, sometimes by the same Mexican workers using similar mechanical equipment. The nature of this flow is such that the direct contribution to the economy of the border towns is negligible, except in the specific case of towns on the path of railroads or highways such as Laredo, Nogales, etc. In such towns a few jobs are generated for office workers, warehousemen, packers, and service fields related to trucking, primarily on the U.S. side of the border.[13]

Tourism is the main "industry" of the Mexican border zone. It is one of the most important "industries" of Mexico as well. Tourist dollars are the main source, directly or indirectly, of the personal income of most residents of the border towns. It is tourism that gives to the gaudy commercial enterprise the glaring predominance over other aspects of economic life and is, therefore, the most immediately perceivable element of economic life in the border towns of Mexico. Tourism, despite its arguable merits as an "industry" in a developing country, has been intensely promoted by the Mexican government in the border area, and this policy cannot be separated from the external financial situation of the country as a whole.

The border zone received 58 million visitors in 1970, who spent an average of fifteen dollars per person. Global border tourist spending in that year, amounting to $880 million, was the second most important item in the current account income of Mexico's balance of payments. The most important trading centers are *Tijuana, Mexicali, Ciudad Juárez, and Nuevo Laredo, which jointly accounted for 80 percent for all border income in 1970.* Although Tijuana is the most commercially active city, it is also the one with the highest level of outgoings, mainly as a result of the illegal import of goods and services by locally based companies, contraband, and the repatriation of profits and dividends by U.S. companies operating in the city. The phenomenon has become increasingly marked; income from 1965 to 1970 increased at an annual 18 percent and the outflow by 20 percent. The balance of border transactions in Ciudad Juárez from 1965 to 1970 moved down at a mean annual 4.4 percent, due to the slow rate of income expansion rate of expenditures (17.5 percent yearly). Mexicali is the second most important city in volume of income and outflow, and third as regards the balance. Income in Mexicali has grown steadily, with constant fluctuations in the outflow. Nuevo Laredo in 1970 accounted for 5 percent of total border transaction income and 5.5 percent of all outflow, contributing 4 percent to the national trade balance.

One last form of economic domination manifested in the border area is the phenomenon of technological dependence. To illustrate the situation I shall use the case of Monterrey, a major Mexican city which is not *on* the border, but whose proximity to the border makes it part and parcel of the whole "border syndrome." Monterrey has been primarily an industrial city, characterized by large scale industry since the 1890s. The natives of Monterrey have been favorably compared (apparently because of their "entrepreneurial spirit") with the Antioqueños of Colombia. The continuing growth of this city has come to depend, more and more, not on the talent and capacity for "self-sacrifice" of the local bourgeois class but on their utilizing, and becoming dominated by, the technology and facilities of U.S. corporations.

Technological dependence manifests itself in at least three fundamental ways. The first is the utilization by U.S.-located firms of some of the technically-skilled manpower which abounds in Monterrey (such as engineers, draftsmen, etc.) to work in the research and development of plants, machinery, blueprints, etc. Final sale of the product is in the United States, and the purchasing parties are charged as if all labor services had been performed at U.S. wages. The other side of the coin is the use by Mexican firms of technical advice and direction from special U.S. consultants to produce cheaper—and technically inferior—plants for production processes in Mexico. Secondly, industrial production in Monterrey has become increasingly dependent on the importation of entire used automated plants. This phenomenon, which is not exclusive to Monterrey or Mexico by any means, can be easily characterized as the "institutionalization of uneven technological development" between the United States and Mexico. Lastly, the two problems described above make it easier for other economic activities dependent upon the United States, such as wholesale distribution of imported machinery, to settle in Monterrey, rather than in other areas. The reason is that Monterrey's wholesale importers have more direct access to manufacturers' representatives than wholesale importers do in other areas. Thus domination breeds further domination.

Illegal Economic Activity

The economic complement of the above technical and economic flows, which give life to the border towns on both sides of the line, is the presence of a variety of illegal (or semilegal) activities. One has been historically inseparable from the border region: smuggling. As in times past, smuggling of goods to either side of the border is commonplace. The better known smuggled items are a variety of narcotic drugs that are transported from Mexico to the U.S.

Prior to World War II, the illicit market in the United States was the recipient of heroin and other opium derivatives[14] from various areas of the world. The Balkans, Turkey, and Persia accounted for considerable quantities. In the Far East, China and India were the principal suppliers. Opium grown in Mexico was less important. The laboratories which transform the opium into heroin were also geographically scattered. World War II brought about important changes in the patterns of trade with the United States. Shipping routes were affected by the war at sea and access to processing laboratories was denied by the war in Europe and the Far East. These war-caused restrictions did not, of course, apply to Mexico. An extensive common border and a heavy flow of automotive traffic between the U.S. and Mexico provided ready access to a limited crude opium supply being produced in the states of Sinaloa, Chihuahua, Durango, and Jalisco. The war-time demands for Mexican opium provided an incentive for increased production by Mexican growers. Today, consequently, it is estimated that Mexican opium is the major source of opiates currently being consumed in the United States' southwest.[15]

Heroin from France currently provides 80 percent of the United States heroin supply. French heroin production relies wholly on opium diverted from government-controlled crops in Turkey—which represents the major source of opium produced for the legitimate pharmaceutical industry in Europe and North America. Some noncontrolled fields are also producing for the illegal market. The illicit Turkish opium moves through several complicated routes which include Syria, Lebanon, and Corsica to France, where it is processed into heroin and shipped to the underworld in the United States through a web of channels and connections.[16]

The traffic in Mexican heroin, in contrast to the French operation, is not organized to any great degree. Usually it is carried on by numerous small operators located on or near the United States border, who cater to individual distributors in Texas, New Mexico, Arizona, and California. Aside from heroin, other drugs have flowed and continue to flow northward from Mexico: marijuana, cocaine, "dangerous drugs," etc. While the U.S. drug market may in itself be an interesting subject of study, its over-all economic impact on border residents and wage-workers is far less important than publicity —such as that obtained through Gordon Liddy's* Operation Intercept in 1970—would lead one to believe.

Less publicized, but probably more important from an economic standpoint, is the contraband into Mexico. According to popular sources, the amount of smuggling is substantial. Many commodities brought into the border area under a variety of arrangements become contraband to be taken into the interior of Mexico. To the extent that smuggling exists, it defeats the protectionist policies of the Mexican government designed to promote "national" industry. Unfortunately, there is no data on which to base a reasonable judgment of the effects of smuggling on the border towns or on Mexico as a whole.[17]

Far more important in the economic fabric of the border towns is the prostitution "industry." The commercial, *non-industrial* character of most Mexican border towns makes them unable to provide employment for the masses of people that overflow into them. Such conditions drive the men into a variety of menial "service" occupations (shoeshine boys, etc.) and it forces women into prostitution. That this "business' is far from being fortuitous and disorganized is revealed by an estimate that places the total of *municipal revenues* for Ciudad Juárez derived from official prostitution at one million dollars per year, or half the total city revenues.[18] The economic domination of the United States economy over the Mexican economy is given an air of pestilence by the relation that exists between a thriving prostitution industry and the presence of tens of thousands of U.S. servicemen in bases along the border. The problem that arises from the quartering of soldiers and the need to provide for relief to their sexual needs is solved by "shifting" it over to the "lower forms of life" of Mexico. Again,

*Of Watergate fame. An account of Gordon Liddy's leading role in Operation Intercept, see "Gordon Liddy: He Bungled into the White House," *Rolling Stone*, July 19, 1973, San Francisco.

there is hardly anything new about this: the Brownsville incident over fifty years ago offered proof of the convenient "outlet" provided by Mexican women for the physiological needs of U.S. soldiers.*

Mexican Remedies

Under the combined stress of demographic explosion and economic deterioration, the Mexican government attempted in 1961 to institute a special effort to integrate its border region with the rest of the nation. The Programa Nacional Fronterizo (PRONAF) was begun in 1961. It provided some infrastructure in the way of buildings, paved roads, industrial parks with electricity and water, etc. This infrastructure was supposed to facilitate and promote the appearance of "import substitution" and the increase of the "tourist industry." Although PRONAF met with initial success it soon became apparent that it would not suffice to meet the unemployment situation in the area, so in 1965 the Mexican government established the Border Industrial Program (BIP) which came into full operation in 1967.

The BIP has received glorious publicity by both Mexican and American official sources.† And the Mexican government has reacted to what has been the clearest result of the BIP: the intensification of the economic dependence of the border towns upon the American economy. It has done so by means of a whole new program which purports to reintegrate the border economy into the national economy of Mexico. Since this new program (The Inter-Ministerial Commission for the Economic Development of the Northern Border Zone and Free Zones) is of recent vintage, not much in the way of data is

*The soldiers in that particular incident were black American soldiers. Would it be a surprise to find that at that time and for many years most U.S. Army Negro units were stationed near the Mexican border?

† See the chapter on the BIP in this book.

available. Thus the best that can be said is that perhaps it is too early to tell. However, a cursory examination of the various dispositions regulating this new program show that its two fundamental policies are: a) a program of duty-free imports of "enticement articles" presumably unavailable to Mexican residents on the Mexican side of the towns and b) the same aid extended for the import of machinery, materials, and equipment needed for the construction, operation, expansion, and maintenance of trade centers. The success of the first aspect of the program means that Mexican wage earners will no longer have to cross the border line to make special purchases since now the Mexican retailer himself can do it duty-free. The second aspect of the program is a rehash of the ISI policies discussed earlier. I fail to see how the program can have any direct effect upon either the massive unemployment and underemployment problem of the border or upon the domination of the economy of this area by the United States economy. Quite the contrary, in the light of the whole of the previous analysis, it would seem that this program, alone or pursued in conjunction with the BIP, will make matters *worse* in the long run.

The Border Syndrome

The border towns have become famous among people throughout Mexico for having the highest wage scales in the entire Republic. As a result, an increasing number of peasants in the interior are making the decision to sell their homes, their cattle, and whatever other belongings they may have, in order to migrate to the border area. They go there expecting to find a wonderful job awaiting them. But a very large percentage are disappointed to discover upon arrival the true state of affairs in border towns. The female is fortunate who finds a job in a factory; rarely does a male find one. Great numbers of unemployed peasants are thus stranded in the border towns. Some return to the interior. Most do not. They have nothing to return to—all of their possessions have been sold.

In the border towns, however, there is no "servant problem" or lack of cheap sex. Border towns are characterized by prostitutes, pimps, and demonstrations of every type of sexual perversion imaginable. The material conditions of subjugation to United States' economic interests are reflected in a degenerate atmosphere where people that are already the victims of poverty and oppression are forced by circumstances to become morally and physically degraded. This state of affairs goes on amidst a climate of callousness which does not allow even the traditional, if hypocritical, notions of immorality and shame associated with prostitution to surface. The same insensitivity is manifested in the majority of studies that deal with the border area and border towns: the fact that countless people are reduced to social behavior hardly distinguishable from that of animals appears to be accepted as something inevitable—an attitude quite in keeping with the tendency of modern social science to regard all that is *real* as *necessary*. I have called these historical and contemporary phenomena the border syndrome.

These aspects of the border economy are by no means unique to the border towns. The availability of cheap domestic servants of Mexican nationality—who may live in the border towns—is one of the "attractions" of western living in southern California; prostitution is not solely a border phenomenon but is also the lot of many Mexican women in the United States. The border syndrome therefore is something which does not arise from the nature of an imaginary line or the "character" of a city. It is instead a syndrome whose roots extend deep into the basis of economic exploitation and oppression and is but a reflection—perhaps the most palpably horrendous—of the division of the world between rich and poor nations today.

vii: Border Economy 3: The Border Industrial Program

The one process in the history of the border area which can be most closely identified with the existence of the border line is the development of the area's Border Industrial Program. Interestingly enough, it is through this program that the border area ultimately ceases to be a particular—if not an isolated—instance of economic development, and instead becomes a locus for the manifestation of structures and processes which are at play in the larger world. This is so because the Border Industrial Program is directly related to the appearance of multinational corporations, and to the ebb and flow of Latin America's post-war economic policies.

A multinational corporation "is multinational in the sense that it operates in a number of nations with the purpose of maximizing the profits not of the individual units on a nation-by-nation basis but of the group as a whole."[1] Its appearance and development must, of course, be understood in a context in which the export of capital was already a predominant aspect of international economic relations.

The development of the multinationals provides positive and negative results. Positively, it brings the results of technological advance to backward areas where it helps disintegrate the old organization of the economy. Negatively, it provides neither independence nor equality for the "underdeveloped" world. The international corporation is not very interested in building up the educational and technical skills levels of the nationals of a country falling in the "periphery." An increase in skills and educational levels has long been acknowledged as an important element in the process of economic development, and as such it has been the subject of considerable investment on the part of national governments in the 1950s and 1960s. Given the structure of the multinational corporation, investment in the educational infrastructure may easily result in a "brain-drain" toward the center countries. At its worst, this type of technically skilled migration may meet at the center with unexpected barriers: discriminatory practices based upon ethnic or cultural factors.

The appearance of the multinational corporation is a sign of the passage to collective capitalism and state capitalism. While doing so, it also affects the design for development of a country by its effect on tax capacity. In order to facilitate economic growth, governments must be able to invest in a variety of "infrastructure" investments which range from the educational programs mentioned above, to road paving, electrification, etc. A most important consideration in gauging the ability of a government to support these services is its ability to generate revenues through taxation. And this ability, in turn, will be affected by the multinational corporation's ability to play off particular levels of infrastructural development with given levels of taxation and to move facilities from one country to another. Whereas the national home base of the corporation is able to obtain some corporate revenue through taxation, this possibility is not so certain for poor countries, especially on a long-term basis. Finally, the multinational corporation represents a strong setback to the long-fought economic gains of the labor movement in advanced countries.[2]

The Border Industrial Program represents the entry of the multinational corporation into the economic development of the border area. It also can be viewed as a manifestation of a broad change in the economic policies of Latin American nations, which, not surprisingly, happen to coincide with the "best interests" of the corporation.

Postwar economic thought regarding Latin America by the ideologues of national capitalist development represented a reversal of the policies that had characterized conventional wisdom before World War II. Before 1945, the growth of most Latin American nations was seen as being dependent, according to a harmonious international division of labor, upon the production of primary commodities for more advanced manufacturing countries. The reversal in thought blamed this world-wide division of labor for the slow development of Latin America: "crecimiento hacia afeura" was to be substituted for "crecimiento hacia adentro."

In many politico-economic tracts, the losses in trade suffered by the export-oriented Latin American nations were amply described, and the emerging conclusions—the basis for postwar orthodoxy—were formed. Latin America, if it wished to develop and prosper, must develop its own industries and must become self-reliant. This was to be done by a variety of measures, but the one name that stuck to the policies followed during this period (roughly from 1950–70) was that of "import substitution industrialization," or ISI.

Current economic thinking about the economic lessons of the postwar period for Latin America (and for the rest of the backward nations) is taking the direction of a *new orthodoxy*. The lessons of the postwar period—up to and including the late 1960s—are seen as follows: a) import-substitution policies have outlived their usefulness; b) the unemployment problem of countries in Latin America has remained unabated because of the labor-saving characteristics of both foreign investment and local "import-substitution industries"; and c) planning and control oriented toward national self-development have become obsolete.

The new orthodoxy which is slowly emerging presents the following prescriptions to remedy Latin America's ills: a) import substitution is to be abandoned in favor of policies that promote the export of manufactured goods; b) planning and restrictions are to be deemphasized in favor of a freer utilization of the "market mechanisms" for national development; and c) foreign capital is welcome, but it will be subject to restrictions designed to "guide" its route so that its introduction will benefit the host nation. Mexico is one of the prime countries where these new prescriptions have been adopted. No longer is Mexico oriented to a development pattern tied to concepts of import substitution. President Echeverría indicated in late 1970 that import substitution was not an answer to Mexico's development, and that, additionally, Mexico needed a significantly increased export sector. The notion of "market" in this context implies two different but related ideas: the first is that profit forces should be allowed to operate which might bring foreign companies and investment into Latin America to engage in operations, thereby making international boundaries less of a barrier for "free enterprise." The second idea is that the "effective market" can be improved and its size increased through the medium of economic integration agreements.

In 1965, the Mexican government established the Border Industrial Program (BIP), which came into full operation in 1967. The primary goal of the BIP was "the alleviation of widespread unemployment prevalent along the 2,000 mile common border with the United States." The advantages of the program for Mexico were officially seen as: a) the appearance of new jobs, and larger incomes; b) the introduction of modern methods of manufacturing; and c) the increase in consumption of Mexican raw materials. The idea of establishing the BIP came from the Mexican Secretaryship of Treasury and Public Credit whose first officer, Octavio Campos Salas, had observed American plants assemblying goods for U.S. markets in the Far East.[3]

In his 1965 report to the nation, President Gustavo Díaz Ordaz announced the institution of the program as an answer to the prevalent unemployment on the northern border. This commitment was reaffirmed by Díaz Ordaz in his 1966 Report to the Nation. After setting up operational procedures for the processing of applications of interested companies, the BIP started in 1967 with seventy-two authorized American-owned plants. This number grew to 147 in 1969, and to 330 in 1972. It is estimated that border plants turned out more than $50 million worth of products in 1971, which represented an increase of more than 200 percent over 1969.[4] The BIP ceased to be a "border" program in 1971 when the Mexican government extended it to a twenty-kilometer-wide coastal strip and to the whole country in November 1972 (the so-called "in-bond" industries). In 1973, exports were estimated at approximately $400 million. The vast majority of the plants are located on the area bordering the United States. Major American corporations actively participating in the BIP include Magnavox, Litton Industries, Kimberly-Clark, General Instrument, Memorex, Samsonite, Republican Corporation, Sears & Roebuck, Motorola, and Hughes Aircraft.

The legal structure of the program is as follows. The Mexican government waived its duties and regulations on the importation of raw materials and capital equipment, as well as its restrictions on foreign capital, for foreign-owned plants located anywhere within a 12.5 mile deep strip of land along the U.S.-Mexico border as long as 100 percent of the finished products were exported out of Mexico. Industries which competed with Mexican exports are generally prohibited from participating. According to Mexican labor law, at least 90 percent of the employees must be Mexican citizens, although executives and technical personnel not available in Mexico can be excluded from the calculation of this percentage. If the company operating in Mexico under the BIP imports 100 percent of raw materials and components and exports 100 percent of product, then there are no sales in Mexico and, consequently, there is no corporate income tax, or any other tax associated with profits, sales, or dividends. It is also possible to escape municipal and state taxes, but this is usually negotiated at the local or state level. Foreign national and Mexican corporations with foreign stockholders are not allowed to own land within 100 kilometers of the border. This regulation has not been waived for the BIP and the interested companies are also required to pay the minimum wage for workers. The minimum wage varies along the border to reflect local conditions and is revised upward every two years by the Mexican government.[5]

The chief United States regulation relevant to the program is Section 807 of the Tariff Schedule of the United States:

> Articles assembled abroad in whole or in part fabricated components, the products of the United States which a) were exported in condition ready for assembly without further fabrication . . . c) have not been advanced in value or improved in condition abroad except by operations incidental to the assembly process such as cleaning, lubricating, and painting. . . . A duty upon the full value of the imported article less the cost or value of such products of the United States.[6]

In other words, duties are to be paid only on the value added abroad. In the case of the Mexican assembly operations, the value added is essentially the wages paid to Mexican workers.

The initial purpose of this legislation was to maintain U.S. production by encouraging the use of U.S. components in foreign-made products. The actual result has been to encourage U.S. corporations to utilize low-wage unskilled labor in "underdeveloped" countries in the assembly of products for the U.S. market. This system exists not only in Mexico, but also in Hong Kong, Taiwan, Korea, and Haiti.

Economic Background and Scope of the BIP

On a more analytical level, the policy decisions establishing and promoting the BIP and its extensions have rested on an analysis of the growth process of the Mexican economy. This analysis showed the Mexican economy to be achieving high raw rates of growth while failing to solve a high unemployment problem as well as a pattern of extreme unevenness in the distribution of income and wealth. While the economy as a whole grew at an average rate of 7 percent a year during the 1960s, underemployment (based on earnings) was estimated to be higher than 50 percent of the labor force in 1970. Another estimate places open unemployment at 2.2 million man-years.[7]

During the 1960s, manufactured goods began to acquire a more important position in Mexico's imports. As has been the case in general with Mexican industrialization, this change was heavily directed toward capital intensive industries. Consequently, the net employment effect of the increase in manufactured exports was fairly insignificant, in part due to the relatively low ratio of employment to output. The promotion of "plantas maquiladoras"—as assembly plants are referred to—was supposed to bring about a structural change in this ratio because of relatively higher labor-intensity. Secondly, the development of assembly plants in specified peripheral areas was seen as part of the national effort to stimulate regional industrialization and to effect a decentralization of production facilities away from major industrial centers, particularly in and around Mexico City.[8]

Since its inception, the BIP has moved with vertiginous speed, but roughly one hundred firms began operating after the Tariff Commission's report became known. Of 147 plants authorized in mid-1969, 103 were in actual operation. The heaviest concentration was in Baja, California, where over seventy plants were assembling U.S.-made components. Of these sixty-eight in Tijuana and Mexicali. The remainder were mainly in Ciudad Juárez, Nuevo Laredo, and Matamoros.[9] Presently, the emphasis is on electronic products and textiles with fully 80 percent of the workers in electronic and textile plants. But many other lines are represented, including dismantling of scrap railroad cars, food processing and packaging, assembly of medical instruments, boats, and caskets.

The usual procedure is to set up two plants: one on each side of the border. Under this "twin-plant" arrangement, the products are initially processed in the U.S. plant, sent to the Mexican counterpart for assembly, and then returned to the American side for "finishing and shipping." The U.S.-side twin is by far the smaller of the plants. It employs very few workers and is designed mainly to fulfill the stipulations of the Tariff Schedule, which presumably requires that the goods be "finished" in the U.S.

> An example of the concept are the "twins of Transitron" an electronic component manufacturer, employing about 75 in Laredo and 1,500 in Nuevo Laredo, Mexico. "Finishing" could mean little

more than pasting on a label. Many plants on the U.S. side hire Mexican residents anyway. Attempts to organize are met by threats to move the rest of the operation to Mexico.[10]

The important centers of the BIP are located, not surprisingly, in "twin-city" locations along the border: San Diego-Tijuana, Calexico-Mexicali, Nogales-Nogales, Douglas-Agua Prieta, El Paso-Ciudad Juárez, Laredo-Nuevo Laredo, etc. Since 1967, the proportion of Section 807 imports coming from Mexico make it the largest foreign assembler of U.S. components for re-export to the U.S. Although wages in Mexico are not as low as in the Far East, the border zone operations have clear advantages over the Far East. The most important are lower transportation costs which can offset the difference in direct wage costs and the facility to supply the foreign plant with machinery and materials other than components.

The expansion of the zones of operation of the assembly plants program was encouraged from the beginning by the American business community in Mexico as evidenced by the following citation:

> Another idea that is rapidly making headway . . . is that of extending the Border Industrialization Program (meaning . . . plants which must export 100 percent of their production) to other areas of the country particularly those which have high job demand and little industry. Already ranked high as possibilities for such a program are the states of Yucatan and Aguascalientes.[11]

Success or Failure?

The performance of the BIP is best examined by analyzing the evidence against the proposed goals ("benefits for Mexico") in the areas of employment, income, technical training, and dollar inflow.

Employment. According to data prepared by the Mexican government, by January 1970 the BIP had created a total of seventeen thousand jobs. At the beginning of 1972, the number was closer to thirty thousand jobs. Although this may seem impressive in absolute figures, it is hardly a solution to the unemployment problem. To adequately evaluate the effect of the BIP on employment, it is necessary to digress for a moment to consider the causes of unemployment in the border area.

The region usually referred to as Northern Mexico is made up of six states: Baja California, Sonora, Chihuahua, Coahuila, Nuevo León, and Tamaulipas. Characteristics of these northern states that became pronounced in the early 1960s were: a) the growth of trade, tourism, and some manufacturing had produced such a large concentration of people in urban centers that the area had become the *most urban* of Mexico; and b) the area had a higher population growth than any region of comparable size had had in Mexico since 1940 (see Tables 15 and 16).

Three important demographic changes converged to bring

TABLE 15

Population Increases and Urban Proportions of Mexico and the Northern Border States, 1949–1970
(Thousands)

| | Northern Border States | | Nation | |
	Totals	% Urban	Totals	% Urban
1940 Population	2,618		19,654	35%
1950 Population	3,763		25,791	43%
1940–50 % Increase	44%		31%	
1960 Population	5,541	64%	34,923	51%
1950–60 % Increase	47%		35%	
1970 Population	8,671		49,561	58%
1960–70 % Increase	57%		42%	

Source: Nathan L. Whellen, "Population Growth in Mexico," *Report of the U.S. Select Commission on Western Hemisphere Migration* (Washington, 1968), pp. 173–184.

TABLE 16

Population Increases in Northern Mexico, 1940–1970

	1940–50 % Increase	1950–60 % Increase	1960–70 % Increase	Projected 1970 Population (Thousands)
Baja California	187	129	112	1,105
Sonora	40	53	61	1,258
Chihuahua	36	44	54	1,892
Coahuila	31	26	33	1,209
Nuevo León	36	46	58	1,704
Tamaulipas	56	43	47	1,504
Regional Totals	44	47	57	8,672
National Totals	31	35	42	49,561

Source: See Table 15.

about these circumstances: the increase of births over deaths, the rural-to-urban shift, and the migration northward. Obviously there are important rural-to-urban as well as south-to-north "pull" factors which cannot be separated from the proximity and economic influence of the United States. Perhaps the most important economic factor is the higher wage rate obtainable in the border states. But it is also important to remember that Latin America has the highest rate of population growth of any of the major underdeveloped regions and that Mexico has the highest rate of population growth in Latin America.

The population increase of the border area has brought with it an unemployment problem. Since 1940, the population of the border states has quadrupled, but jobs have not kept up with the inflow of workers. The closing of the bracero program in 1965 exacerbated the unemployment situation because many braceros who could no longer work in the U.S. chose to remain in northern Mexico instead of returning to their points of origin elsewhere in Mexico. In 1966, unemployment statistics estimates "ran as high as 40-50 percent in several border cities." The incidence of underemployment in the agricultural sector was considered substantial, although reliable figures were not available. At this time, estimates showed three-fourths of the labor force engaged in agricultural pursuits. *The fact that the BIP has further stimulated this migration has already been noted. The employment situation may very well worsen as a result of further migration.*[12]

It is also important to specify the structural differences between unemployment in northern Mexico and the jobs provided by the BIP. Mexican government reports indicate that the sectors of the working force that are hardest hit by unemployment are young men and male heads of households. By contrast, women workers constitute the bulk of the labor employed by the BIP. Roughly, between 65 and 90 percent of the jobs are available for women. In one location (Agua Prieta), *more* than 90 percent of the employed workers are women. The kind of tasks in which women are engaged can be gleaned from the following citation about Rey-Mex Bra, a brassiere-making plant in Reynosa (McAllen), Texas:

> The production supervisor is in charge of hiring women and all are given a dexterity test which judges agility of fingers as well as mental reaction concerning sewing. Testing is based upon elapsed time and varies from operation to operation in the bra-making procedure which involves 22 separate steps on a sewing machine. Quality rather than quantity is being stressed at the plant as trainees are individually trained in one of the 22 steps. Following training, each employee will be expected to turn out three dozen bras per day for production of approximately 6,000 bras daily from the Reynosa plant when full employment is reached.[13]

A third crucial qualification that must be made to the "employment benefits" of the BIP is what traditional economists refer to as "seasonal employment"; i.e., there is no way of telling for how long an authorized plant will remain in actual operation. An indication of the "rate of attrition" in the BIP is given by the comment below:

> It was difficult to get an up-to-date list from any sources because of the constant movement of the companies. The lists provided by the

government offices were used as a starting point for visits, but it was found that many of the plants listed had already closed down and others, not included, had opened up. The greatest attrition was in the Tijuana area. Since Norris & Elliot made their last survey in November 1967, almost 50 percent of the companies then covered had closed their doors.[14]

Thus, in the first two years of the program, the rate of attrition was 50 percent. And predictions about the long-range employment effects of the BIP are vitiated by the typical "slash-and-burn" procedure of capitalist enterprise in backward countries. One hypothetical explanation for this attrition is that U.S. firms may undertake operations south of the border in order to postpone the necessity to scrap existing production methods in favor of more efficient techniques. Utilizing the lower wage costs of Mexican labor allows U.S. firms to ease the costs of switching to more capital intensive operations. Once the new equipment is installed, the need for low-wage labor power goes down, and the firms retreat back over the border leaving even greater numbers of Mexican workers unemployed and requiring more welfare assistance on the part of the Mexican government. Another hypothetical explanation would relate fluctuations in BIP to the relative economic stability of the "mother firm" in the U.S. Unfortunately, the data to test these hypotheses is unavailable at this time.

Income. The above characteristics of the employment produced by BIP are reflected in the income accruing to workers: *an intermittent source of low income accruing to female members of households.* Why a *low* income? It is well-known that since the Mexican revolution, the Mexican government has made a public commitment to maintaining a measure of social welfare as a mode of ensuring political stability. Several "analysts" have pointed to these social measures (especially minimum wage legislation) as one of the constraints upon, if not the main explanation for, the persistence of unemployment in backward areas.[15] In the Mexican BIP, high minimum wages have been unimportant because even though companies are required to pay wages 50 percent above the prevailing minimum wage rates to full-time workers, they are permitted to pay only *half the legal minimum* to on-the-job trainees. According to a Chamber of Commerce paper aimed at U.S. businessmen, one of the "bright spots" of the Mexican labor market is that "the definition of the training period tends to be liberal." How liberal is indicated by an interview with a Mexican girl who has been working for more than seven months for a firm in Nuevo Laredo and is still receiving half wages!

In the northern cities of Mexico, the daily wage is about equal to the American hourly rate, not allowing for on-the-job training liberality (see Table 17). It has been suggested that this

TABLE 17

Comparative Minimum General Salaries on
Assembly Plant Areas of Mexico

	1972-1973 *Dollars per Day*
BAJA CALIFORNIA	
Ensenada	4.308
Mexicali	4.308
Tecate	4.308
Tijuana	4.308
CHIHUAHUA	
Juárez	3.384
SONORA	
Nogales	3.160
TAMAULIPAS	
Nuevo Laredo	3.188
Reynosa	3.188
Matamoros	3.188
YUCATAN	
Merida	2.384

Source: *The Assembly Plants Program in Merida, Yucatan, Mexico* (Merida, 1973).

difference may be partially offset by a productivity difference, but this is not borne out by the evidence. The report of the American Chamber of Commerce quoted above indicates almost universal satisfaction with the performance of Mexican workers. Sixty-one of the sixty-three companies interviewed expressed satisfaction with the performance of Mexican workers and some pointed out that such matters as absenteeism and tardiness—of recent importance in the U.S—were not present in the border zones.

Technical Training. Another area of proposed benefit to Mexico is the training of Mexican workers, but there is little evidence to substantiate the claim that American industries will train Mexicans to replace U.S. managers and technicians. It is certain, at any rate, that *U.S. companies moving to Mexico may import virtually as many skilled workers as wanted.* Also, the utility of the technical training that comes out of BIP is dubious, for if older equipment can remain at least temporarily competitive when used by cheap Mexican labor, a number of firms locating in Mexico may find it advantageous to put new equipment into their U.S. operations and to use the old equipment in the Mexican operations. What this means is that even if Americans train a significant number of Mexicans, and even if Mexican industry comes to be in a position to capitalize on a source of semiskilled workers, many Mexican workers will be trained to work only in obsolete production methods.

Dollar Inflow. To the extent that American firms are paying Mexican workers, the result is a net dollar inflow into Mexico. However, it appears that "U.S. businessmen along the border like the program because over half of Mexican factory workers' wages . . . are spent on this side of the river."[16] Some estimates place the percentage of income spent by Mexicans on the U.S. side of the border at 40 percent. This represents, of course, the percentage of all income spent by all Mexicans in the U.S. zone. One specific study estimates that 39 percent of the BIP's workers' salaries are spent in the U.S.[17]

In summary, little can be said about the net effect on the

balance of payments of both countries. The total earnings of the plants are not known, nor are the total spent in the U.S., or the extent of U.S. sales to equip and supply plants in Mexico. Furthermore, we do not know the extent to which Americans substituted products of Mexican plants for goods previously bought in other countries or, conversely, the extent to which Mexican-American imports increased as a result of the improved competitive position of American products. There are a great many things unknown about the BIP. In the words of David T. Lopez:

> Exactly which manufacturers are being lured to Mexico is virtually impossible to determine before the fact, and the established plants are as easy to inspect as the Chinese Communist atomic plants. Photographers hired in Laredo, El Paso, and San Diego were all unable to come up with pictures inside existing plants. They said they were denied permission to enter the plants and shooed away by the guards.[18]

More recently, an official of the U.S. Custom Service has made public that many of the U.S. companies involved in the BIP have been fined for fake duty declarations at the U.S. border. The Service indicated that the alleged violations range from double invoicing and keeping two sets of books to concealing the true value and extent of their operations, to placing too low a value on goods declared for duty at the border. Customs officials felt that fraudulent duty declarations have become so prevalent at U.S. ports of entry that the agency plans to check the books of the 250 plus firms headquartered in the U.S. with border plants in Mexico.

Evaluation. The performance of the BIP, in terms of its proposed official goals, leaves much to be desired. It has had a composite unsubstantial employment record, and it may have, in the long run, reinforced the elements causing unemployment. It has produced an undistinguished record of personal income promotion, and has not been directed to the relief of the specific structural characteristics of the unemployed population of the area. Its contribution to the development of

Mexican "human capital" can best be described as nil, and the total dollar inflow emanating from the program is not clearly ascertainable. Finally, various sets of provisions protect BIP from almost any kind of taxation by the host country.

On a different level, BIP was supposed to alter existing output employment ratios in Mexican export manufacturing industries by introducing more labor-intensive technology, since this would contribute to the national effort of industrial decentralization. In terms of the first goal, "all results are not in." The one study that I am aware of concluded that the border industries are only slightly more labor-intensive than the average Mexican manufacturing export industry (127 workers per million dollars as opposed to 117 workers).[19] Beyond this, there is a reason to suspect the quality of official information on the actual production of border industries. Secondly, it would be misguided to view the development of the border industries as a farsighted effort to remedy the problem of urban congestion and industrial concentration around the Federal District. Between 1950 and 1960, the rates of growth of the three largest border cities—Mexicali (126 percent), Ciudad Juárez (111 percent), and Tijuana (153 percent)—far surpassed that of Mexico City (60 percent). Urban growth on the border constituted a "problem" before the BIP was instituted; the latter is therefore to be viewed partly as a short-run, stop-gap measure designed to alleviate rising unemployment.

In terms of the political and economic relationships of northern Mexico to the rest of the country, the BIP has signified an abandonment of the traditional Mexican policy of strengthening the local border economy against American business encroachment, and establishing ties of dependence between the northern area and the rest of Mexico. From the establishment of the Zona Libre in the nineteenth century, to the development of colonization projects for Baja California in the 1920s, and the institution of a border policy of the National Border Program (PRONAF) in the early 1960s, the governmental policy of the Mexican state was consistent in its application of a border policy of *containment* regarding the northern colossus (U.S.) and the *integration* of the Mexican border into the national economy. The existence of the Border Industrial Program constitutes an abandonment of this hope for Mexican national economic integration.

In the context of the change of policies by Latin American countries, what is the meaning of the border industries? The BIP is obviously a paradigm of a new panacea. It represents: a) the abandonment of import substitution in industrialization, b) changing emphasis favoring the workings of "the market," c) the "skillful manipulation" of foreign capital, and d) the development of economic integration across national boundaries. If the BIP is representative of the general results of the new panacea, the prospects for Latin America, as well as for the border area, are bleak. Finally, organized labor in the United States has been opposed to the existence of the Border Industrial Program since its inception, and this opposition has come through official publications and official declarations of the leadership of the AFL-CIO. It is the correct view of the AFL-CIO that the BIP is another instance of "runaway plants" being established where labor is not organized and paying wages abysmally low by U.S. standards at the cost of increased unemployment in the U.S. In this view, the BIP constituted the most dangerous "loophole" to minimum wage legislation in the United States.

Nothwithstanding the above, the extent to which organized labor in the United States can exert enough pressure to limit and control the expansion of the BIP is limited by the role which organized U.S. labor has played as a partner in international adventures with the U.S. government. The leadership of organized labor has supported the foreign policy of the State Department since Gompers. And the relationship between the foreign policy of the State Department and the interests of the American corporation has been close. Thus organized labor is left in the paradoxical situation of standing up for imperialism and its necessary foreign policy. This explains the lack of enthusiasm with which organized labor has thus far protested against the BIP.

The analysis ¡ resented in this chapter utilized the relatively abundant amount of data on the BIP that was available in its early years. In recent years data has been rather scanty perhaps because the program has not had the often prognosticated results and because the 1974–75 economic recession has effectively eliminated some of the market for the products of the "maquiladoras." Also, it appears that the "unspoiled workforce" which lured companies to the border ten years ago has undergone some changes; thus North American companies in Mexico feel that "Mexican labor today—as did U.S. labor a few years ago—is killing the goose."[20] In fact, many feel that the goose is already dead and that it is only a matter of time before the border cities become ghost towns. Thus, between October 1974 and April 1975, thirty-nine U.S.-owned assembly plants closed down operations along the Mexican border, while many others cut their work force by as much as 50 percent. More than twenty-three thousand workers were laid off in less than ten months with employment down by 30 percent in Tijuana and Mexicali.[21]

Conclusion

How does the study of the history of the border help in understanding the present conditions of this area and what light does it shed upon its future? In my mind the study of the past is necessary to understand the present and to be able to change the future. The conception of the "border region" as a separate entity, i.e., a unique region that extends to the north and south of the international boundary line, has become a current notion for discussion and investigation. I intend to show the extent to which the previous analysis sheds light upon the validity of that conception. At the same time, I will try to clarify the basis upon which such a conception becomes appropriate to understand the future, i.e., the forces at work at the present time which tend to accelerate or retard the development of the border area as a separate, sui generis region. In doing so I will refer to such conceptions as "borderlands," "Southwest," "border region," "Aztlán," "Chicano colony" and "Chicano nation."

It is clear, from a variety of vantage points, that the border area stands up as unique not because of a developing pattern of homogeneity but, quite the contrary, because of the heterogeneity and diversity of the area. This is so whether we view the border area from economic, linguistic, or broadly defined cultural angles. In terms of the presence of different modes of social economy, one finds in the Sonoran Desert, for instance, the coexistence at the present time of hunters and gatherers, peasant agriculturists, and capitalist industrial urban centers. Diversity is also dominant in terms of the multiplicity of languages spoken by the various ethnic groups that inhabit the area. Thus, in a formal sense heterogeneity and diversity are fundamental to any basis of unity one finds in the border area.

The relative obscurity and paucity of data is a major obstacle to understanding the border area. This is true whether the information sought is historical, economic, or geographical. Whatever period or angle of approach is used, the attempt to provide an analysis and interpretation of the region has of necessity to be based on relatively scanty direct information. There are two distinct aspects to the problem. While much untapped data is known to exist in libraries and repositories throughout Mexico and the United States, scholars have only recently begun the sifting and weighing of this material. Secondly, few works have been devoted *directly* to the border region as such. This is evident in that there is only one bibliographical work devoted to sources for study of the border region.[1]

The definition of "border region" implied in this chapter is not exactly the same as the idea of the "Spanish borderlands" used earlier. "Border region" implies a larger territory than that comprised by the "Spanish borderlands." The concept of the "Spanish borderlands" has most commonly been utilized to describe that territory which is now part of the United States which was at a former time occupied and under the control of either the Spanish crown or the Republic of Mexico. However, this is not always the manner in which the notion of "Spanish borderland" is used; sometimes it is meant, in a very inclusive manner, to encompass all those territories north of the Mexican plateau that were known as the Provincias Internas. In that case it is possible to detect a close resemblance, territorially speaking, between the notions of "Spanish borderlands" and "border region." The latter must also be distinguished from the notion of the "Southwest" which has as many territorial definitions as there are writers on the subject, the geographic range covered in the literature being so narrow as to include only New Mexico and as broad as to include not only New Mexico, Arizona, California, and Texas, but Oklahoma as well. Equally distinct from the "border region" is the conception of "Aztlán" which enjoys much current popularity.

Common to both "borderlands" and "Southwest" history is emphasis upon the study of Spanish language, architecture, clothing, food, religion, etc. Some of the leading exponents of these fields of history have been also concerned with the study of the social institutions that were peculiar to the Spanish and Mexican civilizations that once occupied the area. Because of this concentration of "borderlands" and "Southwest" history, much of the available literature has been tinged, with notable exceptions, by at best a good deal of ethnocentrism and at worst a very backward form of racism. It is also unfortunate that some of the recent literature that has sought to set the historical record straight on the heritage of the Spanish-speaking people has fallen into the same trap of "culturism." The understanding of the historical development of this region should be something more subtle and complex than a polemic about which of the "cultures" represented in the area is superior.

The concept of culture central to the notions of "borderlands," "Southwest," and "Aztlán" is of little use in defining the basis for unity of the border region. Because this concept is widely used in so much of the literature, it is necessary to point out its shortcomings.

The utilization of a general notion such as "culture" by itself is not helpful for the purpose of defining a region. First of all, it usually refers to culture only in a formal sense, without paying proper attention to the social content of a particular culture. Culture is thus sometimes equated with literature and art, sometimes with the sum of the "values" and "status symbols" of a community of people and sometimes with other aspects of everyday life such as colloquial speech, mannerism, clothing, foods, and the like.

The most important aspect of any "culture" should be, however, the manner in which a society organizes the productive labor of its members. These production relations become crucial in determining many other aspects of the culture including values, literature, art, etc. Equally important for the study of a region is some knowledge of the material level of development of the same, i.e., the kinds of artifacts, material goods, and especially instruments of production that are available to the inhabitants of the region. The material level of development and the relations of production that are most characteristic of a region constitute the basic and most important elements of the social content of any culture and must serve as the foundations for the study of any given social-geographic region.

A definition of culture that is concerned with emphasizing the social content can thus be considered as having two mutually dependent aspects: formal and material. The formal aspects of culture would include such things as ideas (art and science), values, rules of personal behavior, social institutions, and, fundamentally, a given set of social relations in the process of production. The material aspect of culture, on the other hand, would be composed of all artifacts and material goods resulting from human activity in a given society. These two aspects are not separate but interdependent. This is so because what is produced in any given society is not merely a reflection of the physical needs of its members but is also an outgrowth of the values and interests of the group or groups that control the production process.

When seen in this light, it becomes clear that a historical account of "Chicano culture," must include the relations of exploitation that were characteristic of the Mission system in early California, for the failure to do so can result in the formulation of statements that are susceptible to reactionary and backward-looking interpretations. The social content of a culture is the basis upon which it can be said that the "Chicano culture" of today is still characterized by negative aspects. The abstract defense of an imaginary, entirely "good" culture, is nothing but the resurrection of the myth of the noble savage in a different disguise, and it serves to push into the background real differences and to obviate the concern for economic and political equality.

The "border region" should also be distinguished from the

question of whether or not a Chicano "nation" or "colony" exists as a nation within the United States. The question of Chicano nationality itself has on occasion been presented in recent literature in a confused, intertwined manner with the narrow cultural definitions discussed above. The elements that make up a nation are not those that enter into the definition of culture and are not necessarily those that add up to the determination of an economic region.

The concept of nationhood arose during the breakdown of feudal barriers in Western Europe and elsewhere with the development of commodity circulation and home markets and also with the acquisition and recognition of a common language and territory, all of which gave rise to the idea of a national character. Nations so defined may have acquired independence or they may still suffer from oppression from which they want to obtain independence by means of a national movement. Typical cases are the appearance of a variety of nations in Europe several centuries ago, the appearance of the Latin American nations, including Mexico, and the rise of national liberation movements and newly independent nations in the world today.

It is historically documentable that the kinds of economic and territorial unity implied by the concept of nationhood became present in the Spanish southwest only after the appearance of the Old Spanish Trail. This was the first time that there were any trade bonds between the otherwise isolated Spanish settlements of New Mexico and California. Any discussion of the possible existence of a nation in the Southwest, either in the nineteenth century or at the present time, must take as its point of departure the concrete development of commodity circulation in the 1820s. Aside from that, it should be indisputable that questions such as nationality cannot be settled on the basis of abstract norms but must be tied to economics, politics, history, and territoriality. Lastly, the examination of this question must take into account that in the present epoch the boundaries between nations seem subject to erosion. If in its beginnings capitalism provided the impulse for the breakdown of feudal barriers and thus helped form nations, at the present time its continuing development tends to destroy the independent character of nations.

Is it possible to refer to the border region as a nation or colony? In my estimation the answer clearly must be negative for a variety of reasons. In the first place, the border region includes large portions of both urban and rural areas of northern Mexico, in which several million people of Mexican nationality live at the present time. It is easy to make the argument that a large number of these people suffer under a variety of forms of oppression, but it is not possible to claim that their oppression, poverty, etc., has the character of national oppression. Secondly, it is difficult to conceive in what sense the region north and south of the border became an economic unity on the basis of a common economic life. The development of economic relations in this area coincides not with the development of commodity circulation in a "home market" corresponding to its territory but rather with the development of *foreign* economic relations between the United States and Mexico. Thirdly, the territorial region which is implied by the notion of border area is subject to as many geographical interpretations as the notion of the "Southwest." It is clearly not a well-defined territory in the economic and social sense that a nation must be.

Finally, and perhaps, the most important consideration of all, is the historical absence of a political movement of a national character, i.e., towards the formation of an independent national state in this area. A study of the struggles of the nineteenth century reveals that they constituted either struggles led by feudal reactionary elements against the intrusion of capitalism in the Southwest or struggles over the maintenance of communal rights of use and ownership. Even the latter represent struggles for precapitalist forms of organization, which occur precisely because of the savage manner in which the separation of the peasants from communally owned means of production was carried out by the bourgeoisie, but in no way do they represent the struggles of a developing national Chicano bourgeoisie.

The border region is to be defined neither as a culturally

homogeneous area nor as a nation. The bases upon which it is permissible to speak of the area as possessing a degree of cohesiveness are twofold—geographic and economic. In a geographic sense, north and south and across the whole length of the border, a certain homogeneity exists which is bound to influence the character of whatever human developments flourish. These basic geographic features are well known.

The western part of the border from about the thirty-eighth to the twenty-third parallel is essentially a geographic unit. *Climactically*, it is very dry, producing a reliance on massive irrigation for agriculture to prosper. In terms of *geological resources* the border area from the Pacific shores to a line running north to south from the Colorado Rockies to Zacatecas in Mexico has been for centuries (and is today) a rich mining area for copper, silver, gold, lead, tungsten, and several other minerals. *Agriculturally*, the aridity and similar climate of the area resulted in the cultivation of similar crops both north and south of the border. The boundary line runs approximately through the middle of this climactic, geologic, and agricultural area.

Geographic unity is enhanced rather than diminished by such other geographical features as the Sonoran Desert and the Rio Grande (Brave del Norte). In the case of the Sonoran Desert, a vast expanse of arid land which used to effectively divide the western border region has turned, with the development of technology and modern means of communication, into a unifying factor. In a sense it is the ability to deal with the problems peculiar to a desert which provides for such unity rather than further separation. In the eastern part of the border zone, the Rio Grande has also provided for a long time a feature of unification in an otherwise parched area. This is so simply because the Rio Grande is not the kind of torrential river which could ever become a serious obstacle. On the contrary, the history of the area shows that its inhabitants for years had closer contacts with each other that they had with the people of other regions of either the United States or Mexico.

A substantial foundation of economic forces and relations lies on this natural geographical base. These economic connections have already been described in some detail and will not be repeated here. It is necessary to present more explicitly, however, the raison d'être for the peculiar economic dependence between the United States and Mexico as revealed on the border zone.

Economically, the unity that is characteristic of the border region is based upon the uneven development of the areas north and south of the border and as such is ultimately a reflection of the uneven development of the United States and Mexico. The problem of uneven development, or, more correctly, the problem of imperialism, is specific to the twentieth century. Before the onset of the twentieth century, there were nations and territories that had not been brought into the world market. But these were not yet "rich nations" and "poor nations." This distinction appears in the twentieth century with the development of monopoly capitalism, i.e., with imperialism.

The separation of the world into poor nations and rich nations is not a natural sort of phenomenon. The explanation for it lies in the development and growth of monopolistic forms of capitalism in the more economically advanced nations, the ability of these monopoly enterprises to affect the economic life of the less advanced nations and, consequently, the persistence of poverty and backwardness and at best the appearance of warped development possibilities in the poor areas of the world.[2]

The relations of economic domination and dependence which exist between the United States and Mexico are but one concrete example of the general principle about the relationship of domination and dependence which exist between advanced countries and poor countries. As such, the basis of the economic unity of the border is founded on inequality, uneven development, and domination.

Can unbalanced, irrational growth provide the basis for the future integration of an area into some sort of formal economic region? The answer must once again be negative. The apparent economic unity of the border area cannot be seen in separation from the inability of the Mexican economy to provide adequate employment for millions of people who must therefore seek jobs in the United States as illegal workers. Rational economic development for Mexico must entail the ability to utilize these millions of human beings in productive occupations in their homeland. But this possibility is unrealizable for Mexico short of drastic economic planning and a restructuring of the economic fabric of its society. Even if it were possible to achieve such a change in Mexico, the absence from the United States's Southwest of several million workers could not be achieved short of important changes in the economic structure of the United States.

Even in the highly monopolized and state-directed economy of the United States, profit considerations will always pose some limits to the development of a truly integrated plan for the Southwest—a plan that can allow for a genuine economic development of Mexico and that can make the Southwest economy independent of such a large pool of cheap labor. Thus, to speak of a border economic regional unit *as we know it today* can only imply the continuation of the status quo in both the United States and Mexico. A better, more rational economic development future for this geographic area must signify the disappearance of the present economic elements of unity, i.e., the disappearance of imperialism and uneven development.

Notes

I: MATERIAL BASIS OF CULTURE IN THE OLD BORDERLANDS

1. François Chevalier, *Land and Society in Colonial Mexico* (Berkeley and Los Angeles: University of California Press, 1963), p. 157.

2. Robert S. Chamberlain, *Castilian Background of the Repartimiento-Encomienda* (Washington, D.C.: Carnegie Institution, 1939).

3. George I. Sanchez, *Forgotten People: A Study of New Mexicans* (Albuquerque: University of New Mexico Press, 1949), chap. 1.

4. This is a dangerous road: from this ahistorical vantage point, slavery was also benevolent, more so than capitalism.

5. Chevalier, *Land and Society*, chap. 5.

6. O. E. Leonard, *The Role of the Land Grant in the Social Organization and Social Processes of a Spanish-American Village in New Mexico* (Albuquerque: Calvin Horn, 1970), chap. 5.

7. Rodolfo Acuña, *Occupied America* (San Francisco: Canfield Press, 1972), chap. 1.

8. Chevalier, *Land and Society*, chap. 3.

9. William Dusenberry, *The Mexican Mesta* (Urbana: University of Illinois Press, 1963). These generalizations regarding the northern territories do not rule out exceptions.

10. In this context, generalization is geared toward the identification of widespread and predominant patterns, especially those which held on balance the direction of social change.

11. Marshall Sahlins, *Stone Age Economics* (Chicago: Aldine Press, 1972), chap. 1.

12. Karl Kautsky, *La Cuestión Agraria* (Paris: Ruedo Ibérico, 1970), chap. 1.

13. United States Department of Agriculture, Soil Conservation Service, *A Report on the Cuba Valley*, Reg. Bull. No. 36, Cons. Economic

Series No. 9; see also *Tenant Herding in the Cuba Valley,* Reg. Bull. No. 37, Cons. Economic Series No. 10.

14. Livestock raising (whether in the form of sheep or beef cattle) was the most important material element of production during the Spanish and Mexican periods of the Southwest. In New Mexico, grazing sheep gained increasing economic importance from the mid-eighteenth century onward. In other areas, such as California and parts of Texas and Arizona, raising beef cattle became the primary economic activity. The development of livestock in this area formed the basis for the northward expansion of the colonial effort. The spread of Spanish influence, especially its religious impact, has usually been attributed to the presence of large, exploitable resources of precious metals and the resulting development of mining. Popular legend attributes the saying "donde no hay plata, no entra la religión" or "no silver mining, no religious conversion" to a Franciscan. While it is true that during the early stages of conquest, the haciendas and their resources were secondary to mining in economic importance, as northward expansion passed Zacatecas, mining became negligible and cattle raising haciendas became the key to economic sustenance.

15. Exploration of the California coast occurred as early as the sixteenth century, for a variety of reasons ranging from the search for a northward passage to the need for a port of call that would serve as a refuge for Spanish ships against pirates. These early Spanish ships were the famed Manila galleons, returning to Mexico via the California coast loaded with silk, spices, and other products from the Far East. Although Monterey Bay was discovered at this time, it would be over two hundred years before as notable a geographic feature as San Francisco Bay would be discovered.

16. Cecil Alan Hutchinson, *Frontier Settlement in Mexican California: The Híjar-Padrés Colony and Its Origins, 1769–1835* (New Haven: Yale University Press, 1969).

17. Under the domination of the priests, the Indians contributed to the imperial economy of Spain, worshiped as Roman Catholics, and dressed like Europeans. The mission system was utilized to minimize the threat of Indian revolt and to help hold distant frontiers against foreign claims and intrusions. As such, it became an important scheme for defensive colonization.

18. Herbert E. Bolton, "The Mission as a Frontier Institution in the Spanish-American Colonies,"*American Historical Review* 23 (1917/18).

19. Michael P. Costeloe, *Church Wealth in Mexico* (London: Cambridge University Press, 1967).

20. Carey McWilliams, *Southern California Country* (New York: Duell, Sloan & Pearce, 1946), chap. 1.

21. During the early years of missionary activity, Indians were

attracted to the missions by various means of enticement. As the years passed, however, the mission system began to take a large toll of Indian lives. From 1769 to 1833, 29,100 Indian births and 62,000 deaths were recorded by the California missions. As this trend developed, the missionaries—aided by colonial soldiers—conducted a more forceful recruitment by means of raids into "wild" Indian territory.

22. Varden Fuller, "The Supply of Agricultural Labor as a Factor in the Evolution of Farm Organization in California," in Hearings before a Subcommittee of the Committee on Education and Labor, United States Senate, Seventy-Six Congress; Part 54, *Agricultural Labor in California* (Washington, D.C.: Government Printing Office, 1940).

23. Ibid., p. 19787.

24. Lynn Perrigo, *Our Spanish Southwest* (Dallas: New Mexico Highlands University, 1960).

25. Robert Glass Cleland, *The Cattle on a Thousand Hills* (San Marino: The Huntington Library, 1951), chap. 2.

26. Odie B. Faulk, "The Presidio: Fortress or Farce?" *Journal of the West* 3, no. 1 (January 1969).

27. Ernest Mandel, *Marxist Economic Theory* (New York: Monthly Review Press, 1962), vol. 1, chap. 9.

28. Rent-in-kind signifies that the labor of the direct producer for himself and his labor for the landlord are no longer separate.

29. Karl Marx, *Capital*, 3 vols. (New York: International Publishers, 1967), 3:797.

30. Ibid., p. 807.

31. Ibid., p. 798.

32. The argument to the effect that there was feudalism in Europe but *not* in Spain is not an argument at all. This is the case because the very elements that give content to this mode of production—the absence of rapid communication, geographical isolation, and the basic immobility of the source of rent—can only entail differences in the ways in which the mode of production will manifest itself. (In different times and places, the juridical, ideological, and cultural expression of a fundamentally similar mode of economic production can take different forms.) Once this is positively clarified, the argument becomes one over equivocal presentations of the question. The same economic basis can show—because of numerous empirical circumstances, natural environments, racial relations, etc.—infinite varieties and gradations.

33. Jaime Vicens Vives, *Historia de España y América* (Madrid: Grijalbo, 1960), vol. 2, "Feudalism."

34. Marc Simmons, "Settlement Patterns and Village Plans in Colo-

nial New Mexico," *Journal of the West* 8, no. 1 (January 1969).

35. The presidio was a military post designed for provincial defense against foreign invasion, and for the preservation of internal order. The presidio received sufficient land to supply its garrison with food and furnish pastures for the king's cattle, horses, and other livestock. A line of presidios eventually spanned the entire North American continent from Florida to California. Some eventually became towns, as in the case of San Francisco. The presidios were essentially forts; from an institutional point of view, they were predated by a variety of fortifications that spearheaded the advance and protected the retreat of the Spanish in their struggle with the Moors on the Iberian Peninsula. From a wider perspective, they played a negligible part in the economic life of the colonies and dovetailed into the pattern of exploitation of borrowing mission Indians as domestic and field servants.

36. Burl Noggle, "Anglo Observers of the Southwest Borderlands, 1825–1890: The Rise of a Concept," *Arizona and the West* 1 (1959).

37. The development and application of science and technology to agriculture historically occurred with the expansion of capitalism (in the sense of capitalist class relations) to rural areas. This expansion occurred sporadically in most Western nations and usually lagged behind developments in urban, commercial, and industrial capitalism.

In the classical development of the capitalist mode of production, the application of machinery to agriculture has had to overcome more technical obstacles than in urban industry. In urban industry, the working place—the factory—is artificially and conveniently molded to the physical requirements of its machinery; in agriculture, the physical setting is usually the given, and the machinery has to be adapted, which is not always an easy or possible task. In urban industry, machinery represents a larger savings in the use of labor power since machines can be utilized on a 24-hour 365-day schedule; in agriculture, their utilization occurs on a seasonal basis. In terms of human requirements, typical urban industry under capitalism does not demand abilities greater than those possessed by a craftsman. With agricultural machinery, the problem is more complex, since considerable training is often necessary for its correct operation and maintenance. Despite these and other difficulties, the extreme social barrier to capitalist forms of agriculture in Europe, the United States, and South America has been the presence of large landholding monopolies. In this sense, landed property can act as a powerful deterrent to the development of productive forces, because the monopoly exercised over land allows its owners to exact a tribute in the form of rent for making land accessible for modern production.

II: DEVELOPMENT OF COMMODITY CIRCULATION IN THE SOUTHWEST

1. Karl Marx, *Capital,* 3 vols. (New York: International Publishers, 1967), 1: 325–337.

2. Tulio Halperín-Donghi, *The Aftermath of Revolution in Latin America* (New York: Harper & Row, 1973).

3. Max L. Moorhead, *New Mexico's Royal Road, Trade and Travel on the Chihuahua Trail* (Norman: University of Oklahoma Press, 1958), chap. 2.

4. Ibid.

5. Ibid.

6. Richard Henry Dana, *Two Years Before the Mast* (Los Angeles: The Ward Ritchie Press, 1964).

7. Cf. Helen Bank, *California Mission Days* (New York: Doubleday, 1951); also Edwin Corle, *The Royal Highway* (Indianapolis: Bobbs-Merrill, 1949).

8. Vito Alesio Robles, *Coahuila y Texas en la Epoca Colonial* (Mexico: Editorial Cultura, 1938), chap. 41.

9. On this point see, Alicia V. Tjarks, "Comparative Demographic Analysis of Texas, 1777–1793," *Southwestern Historical Quarterly* 5, no. 2, pp. 291–398.

10. For a variety of views on Spanish-South American relations, cf. R. A. Humphreys and John Lynch, eds., *The Origins of the Latin American Revolutions, 1808–1926* (New York: Alfred A. Knopf, 1965).

11. Ibid.

12. John Lynch, *The Spanish-American Revolutions 1808–1826* (New York: Norton, 1973), chap. 9.

13. David J. Weber, *The Taos Trappers: The Fur Trade in the Far Southwest, 1540–1846* (Norman: University of Oklahoma Press, 1968).

14. Robert G. Cleland, *This Reckless Breed of Men* (New York: Alfred A. Knopf, 1963).

15. LeRoy R. Hafen, *The Mountain Men and Fur Trade of the Far West* (Glendale: The Arthur H. Clark Company, 1965).

16. Cf. John Galbraith, "A Note on the British Fur Trade in California," *Pacific Historical Review* 24, no. 3 (August 1955), pp. 253–260; also Dale Morgan, "The Fur Trade and Its Historians," in *The American West* 3, no. 2 (Spring 1966), pp. 28–35, 92–93.

17. Josiah Gregg, *Commerce of the Prairies*, 2 vols. (New York: J. B. Lippincott, 1844).

18. Lynn I. Perrigo, *Our Spanish Southwest* (Dallas: New Mexico Highlands University, 1960), chap. 6.

19. Moorhead, *New Mexico's Royal Road*, chap. 4.

20. Leonard Pitt, *The Decline of the Californios* (Berkeley: University of California Press, 1971), chap. 1.

21. Cf. on this Eleanor Lawrence, "Mexican Trade Between Santa Fe and Los Angeles, 1830–1848," *California Historical Society Quarterly* 10 (March 1931), pp. 27–29.

22. The term "backward" does lead sometimes to regrettable misinterpretations. It is a grave mistake to view the relative low degree of productivity, technology, organization of labor, labor skills, etc. i.e., societal characteristics, as the result of the actions of individuals who are somehow inferior. Nothing is, in fact, further from the truth. For instance, in backward *societies* the low degree of division of labor signifies the ability of each individual member to perform dexterously a large variety of tasks; the opposite is true in advanced societies; so that backward or "simpler" societies are usually composed of individuals who are in a sense more "complex" than modern man because they are so much less interdependent.

23. Raul A. Fernandez and José F. Ocampo, "The Latin American Revolution: A Theory of Imperialism, Not Dependence," in *Latin American Perspectives* 1, no. 1 (1974), pp. 30–61.

III: THE VICTORY OF CAPITALISM

1. Lynn I. Perrigo, *Our Spanish Southwest* (Dallas; New Mexico Highlands University, 1960), chaps. 6–7.

2. Hubert Herring, *A History of Latin America* (New York: Alfred A. Knopf, 1965), chap. 19.

3. Perrigo, *Our Spanish Southwest*, chap. 7.

4. Warren Beck, *New Mexico* (Norman: University of Oklahoma Press, 1962).

5. William Robinson, *Land in California* (Berkeley: University of California Press, 1948).

6. On the question of litigation over Spanish landgrants see Leonard Pitt, *The Decline of the Californios* (Berkeley: University of California Press, 1966); Carey McWilliams, *Factories in the Fields* (San Francisco: Anchor Books, 1969).

7. Paul W. Gates, "Adjudication of Spanish-Mexican Land Claims in California," *The Huntington Library Quarterly*, no. 3 (May 1958); cf. also Paul W. Gates, "California's Embattled Settlers," *California Historical Society Quarterly* 41 (1962).

8. McWilliams, *Factories in the Fields*, chaps. 1–2.

9. Maurice G. Fulton, *History of the Lincoln County War* (Tucson: University of Arizona Press, 1968).

10. Curiously, the converse also applied: in some counties bordering on Mexico, the intense level of conflict served as a protective measure. As late as 1930, supposedly more than 50 percent of the

property owners in Zapata and Cameron counties were the descendants of original Mexican grantees. Cf. Paul S. Taylor, *An American Mexican Frontier* (Chapel Hill: University of North Carolina Press, 1934), chap. 23; Carey McWilliams, *North from Mexico* (New York: Greenwood Publishers, 1968), chap. 6.

11. Robert G. Cleland, *This Reckless Breed of Men* (New York: Alfred A. Knopf, 1963), chap. 7.

12. Ibid., pp. 111–133.

13. Ibid., chap. 7.

14. For an examination of the effects of commerce and usury on the lord's and peasant's economy, cf. Maurice H. Dobb, *Studies in the Development of Capitalism* (New York: International Publishers, 1947), chaps. 2 and 3.

15. Karl Marx, *Capital*, 3 vols. (New York: International Publishers, 1967), 3:595.

16. Glenn S. Dumke, *The Boom of the Eighties in Southern California* (San Marino: The Huntington Library, 1944), chaps. 1–4.

17. Ibid.

18. An excellent study on usury capital practices in New Mexico is William J. Parish, *The Charles Ilfeld Company: A Study of the Rise and Decline of Mercantile Capitalism in New Mexico* (Cambridge: Harvard University Press, 1961).

19. A. David Sandoval, "An Economic Analysis of New Mexico History," *New Mexico Business* 20, no. 2 (February 1967), pp. 1–34.

20. Leonard Arrington, "From Apache-Hunting to Hosting America: The Economic Development of Arizona, 1863–1950," in *Arizona Review* 18, nos. 8–9 (1969), pp. 1–5.

IV: ESTABLISHMENT OF A NEW BORDER

1. Rodolfo Acuña, *Occupied America* (San Francisco: Canfield Press, 1972), chap. 4.

2. Clarence C. Clendenen, *Blood on the Border* (London: Collier-Macmillan, 1969), chaps. 4–5.

3. Charles H. Harris III, *The Sánchez Navarros: A Socio-economic Study of a Coahuilan Latifundio, 1846–1853* (Chicago: Loyola University Press, 1964).

4. On the question of the Free Zone, see Daniel Cosío Villegas, *Estados Unidos contra Porfirío Díaz* (Mexico: Editorial Hermes, 1956); Matías Romero, *Mexico and the United States* (New York: Putnam's Sons, 1898); James M. Callahan, *American Foreign Policy in Mexican Relations* (New York: Cooper Square, 1968), passim.

5. Cosío Villegas, *Estados Unidos*, pp. 282–293.

6. Robert D. Gregg, *The Influence of Border Troubles on Relations Between the United States and Mexico, 1876–1910* (Baltimore: The Johns Hopkins Press, 1937).

7. Fred J. Rippy, "Border Troubles Along the Rio Grande, 1848–1860," *Southwestern Historical Quarterly* 23 (1919).

8. Cosío Villegas, *Estados Unidos*.

9. Eric Hobsbawn, *Bandits* (New York: Dell Publishing, 1969).

10. Carey McWilliams, *Factories in the Field* (San Francisco: Anchor Books, 1969), chap. 5.

11. Gregg, *The Influence of Border Troubles,* p. 45.

V: BORDER ECONOMY 1: THE FRAMEWORK OF MIGRATION

1. Cited in Karl Marx, *Capital*, 3 vols. (New York: International Publishers, 1967), 1:768.

2. Capitalism is defined here as a *mode of production*. This definition is chosen by the author with full cognizance of the existence of alternative definitions of capitalism, i.e., such as those propounded by Max Weber, Adam Smith, etc., which are however incompatible with the methodology used throughout these essays. The interested reader may consult Maurice H. Dobb, *Studies in the Development of Capitalism* (New York: International Publishers, 1964), for a discussion of the usefulness of different definitions of capitalism.

3. Carey McWilliams, *Factories in the Fields*, (San Francisco: Anchor Books, 1969), chap. 7.

4. The term depeasanting refers to the uprooting of the peasant from his landholdings by the expansion of latifundios and other means.

5. Roger Bartra, "Campesinado y poder político en Mexico," *Latin American Perspectives* 2, no. 2 (1975).

6. Max S. Handman, "Economic Reason for the Coming of the Mexican Immigrant," *American Journal of Sociology* 35:601–611.

VI: BORDER ECONOMY 2: URBANIZATION AND BORDER TOWNS

1. An excellent analysis of the structural characteristics of the Mexican economy is presented by various authors in "Mexico: The Limits of State Capitalism," a special issue on Mexico of *Latin American Perspectives* 2, no. 2, in which this author served as issue editor.

2. Michael W. Gordon, "The Contemporary Mexican Approach to Growth with Foreign Investment: Controlled But Participatory

Independence," *California Western Law Review* 10, no. 1 (Fall 1973), p. 4.

3. David Barkin, "Mexico's Albatross: The United States Economy," *Latin American Perspectives* 2, no. 2.

4. Ibid., p. 72.

5. Edmundo Sánchez Aguilar, *Mexico: deuda externa y operacion de la banca privada americana*, translation of doctoral thesis (Cambridge: Harvard University Press, 1973).

6. Albert O. Hirschman, *The Strategy of Economic Development* (New Haven and London: Yale University Press, 1958), chap. 7.

7. Albert O. Hirschman, "The Political Economy of Import-Substituting Industrialization in Latin America," *Quarterly Journal of Economics*, February 1968.

8. 'C. V. Vaitsos, "Transfer of Resources and Preservation of Monopoly Rents," Center of International Affairs, Harvard University, *Economic Development Report 168* (1970).

9. Eugene Keith Chamberlin, "Mexican Colonization versus American Interests in Lower California," *Pacific Historical Review* 20 (1951): 43–55.

10. *Los Angeles Times*, November 26, 1974.

11. Jerry R. Ladman and Mark O. Paulsen, *Economic Impact of the Mexican Border Industrialization Program: Agua Prieta, Sonora*, Center for Latin American Studies (Tempe, Arizona, 1972), p. 40.

12. David S. North, *The Border Crossers* (Washington, D.C.: Transcentury Corporation, 1970), p. 46.

13. "Winter Vegetables in Mexico," *Foreign Agricultural Circular*, July 28, 1960; Craig L. Dozier, "Mexico's Transformed Northwest," *Geographical Review*, October 1963.

14. The narcotic drug scene in the United States has been unquestionably dominated over the years by the opium alkaloid, diacetyl morphine, commonly known as heroin. This observation is based on an analysis of recent statistics by the Federal Bureau of Narcotics which indicated that for 93 percent of the recorded addicts, heroin is the drug of choice.

15. George H. Gaffney, "Narcotic Drugs—Their Origin and Routes of Traffic," *Drugs and Youth, Rutgers Symposium on Drug Abuse, Rutgers University, 1968*, ed. John R. Wittenborn, et al. (Springfield, Illinois: Thomas, 1969), p. 28.

16. A detailed description of the routes of heroin into the United States is available in United States Senate, Committee on Government Operations, *Organized Crime and Illicit Traffic in Narcotics Hearings, 1963–64*, Parts 1–3 and 4–6 (Washington: Government Printing Office, 1965).

17. Timothy King, *Mexico, Industrialization and Trade Policies Since 1940* (London: Oxford University Press, 1970), p. 80.

18. Patrick H. McNamara, "Prostitution along the U.S.-Mexico Border: A Survey," *Border-State University Consortium for Latin America*, Occasional Papers, no. 2.

VII: BORDER ECONOMY 3: THE BORDER INDUSTRIAL PROGRAM

1. Harry Magdoff and Paul Sweezy, "Notes on the Multinational Corporation," in *Readings in U.S. Imperialism,* ed. K. T. Fann and D. C. Hodges (Boston: Sargent, 1971).

2. Ibid.

3. Ralph S. Jackson, Jr., *The Border Industrialization Program of Northern Mexico.* Seminar in Latin American Commercial Law, The University of Texas Law School, Fall, 1968. Lic. Jorge Farías Negrete, *Industrialization Program for the Mexican Northern Border* (Mexico: Banco Comercial Mexicano, 1969).

4. "Big Deal at the Border," *Newsweek,* January 24, 1972.

5. Jerry R. Ladman and Mark O. Paulson, *Economic Impact of the Mexican Border Industrialization Program: Agua Prieta, Sonora,* Special Study no. 10, Center for Latin American Studies, Arizona State University, (Tempe, Arizona, 1972).

6. Benjamin J. Taylor and M. E. Bond, "Mexican Border Industrialization," *MSU Business Topics,* Spring 1968, p. 36.

7. Andrés Caso, "El empleo como objetivo del desarrollo," *Trimestre económico,* April-June 1971. Also see several studies cited by Susume Watanabe, "Constraints on Labour-Intensive Export Industries in Mexico," *International Labour Review* (January 1974), 109:23–45.

8. A. M. Lavell, "Regional Industrialization in Mexico: Some Policy Considerations," *Regional Studies* 6 (1972): 343–362.

9. Federal Reserve Bank of San Francisco, "Factories on the Border," *Monthly Review,* December 1971.

10. David T. Lopez, "Low-wage Lure South of the Border," *AFL-CIO American Federationist,* June 1969, p. 2.

11. "Border Industries Foster New Jobs, More Exports," *Mexican-American Review,* February 1968, p. 14.

12. Taylor and Bond, "Mexican Border Industrialization," p. 36; Anna-Stina Ericson, *Labor Developments Abroad* (Washington, D.C.: U.S. Department of Labor, June 1967), p. 16; Federal Reserve Bank of San Francisco, "Factories on the Border," p. 215.

13. *The Monitor,* McAllen, Texas, January 4, 1970.

14. American Chamber of Commerce of Mexico, A.C., *Survey on Border Development Program* (1969).

15. Lloyd G. Reynolds, "Wages and Employment in a Labor-Surplus Economy," *American Economic Review,* March 1965, pp. 19–39; Ian Little, Tibor Scitovsky, Maurice Scott, *Industry and Trade in*

Some Developing Countries: A Comparative Study (London: Oxford University Press, 1970).

16. *The Monitor*, McAllen, Texas, May 21, 1969, p. 3a.

17. Ladman and Paulson, *Economic Impact*, p. 50.

18. David T. Lopez, "Low-wage Lure South of the Border," *AFL-CIO American Federationist*, June 1968, p. 2.

19. *New York Times*, December 6, 1970, p. 23, col. 1.

20. Cited in "Hit and Run, U.S. Runaway Shops on the Mexican Border," *NACLA's Latin America and Empire Report* 9, no. 5 (July-August 1975).

21. The best analysis of the recent disenchantment of the multinationals with present border conditions is given in the *NACLA* report cited in note 20.

CONCLUSION

1. Charles C. Cumberland, "The United States-Mexico Border: A Selective Guide to the Literature of the Region," *Rural Sociology* 25, no. 2 (June 1960).

2. Cf. Raul A. Fernandez and José F. Ocampo, "The Latin American Revolution: A Theory of Imperialism, Not Dependence," in *Latin American Perspectives* 1, no. 1.

Index